Curing Coral

A Journey Through Childhood Cancer

By Shane Meader

Copyright © 2013 by Shane Meader

All rights reserved. No reproductions of any form in part or whole allowed without express documented permission from the publisher except for the use of brief quotations in a book review.

Printed in the United States of America

First Printing, 2014

ISBN-10: 1499334591

ISBN-13: 978-1499334593

Published by Shane Meader 2014, Des Moines, Iowa

Dedicated to:

Miss ma'am, Little Miss Peach Pie... Coral Blossom.

... the strange duality of our existence.

Stronger than we ever thought we could be.

Yet powerless and vulnerable.

Supported by more people than we ever knew cared.

Yet alone in our fear.

Our good fortune in the world of pediatric oncology....

And the terribleness of our situation by any other parent's measure.

– Alycia Steinberg 2012

TABLE OF CONTENTS

Foreword ix
Preface xvii
1 Familiar Life 3
2 Oblivious Journey 21
3 Acute Destiny 33
4 Cellular Campaign 51
5 Inevitable Results 83
6 Guarded Victories 117
Chronology 139
Appendix 145
Notes 151
References 157

Foreword

Engineers are all the same.

Or so I thought.

As the treating physician for hundreds of children with cancer, I have had the privilege of taking care of patients and families with diverse cultural, socioeconomic, and educational backgrounds. During a routine visit to the outpatient clinic, some patients simply want to know if things are going well or if they are not. Other patients just want to know if their child can safely play tee ball. Engineers, on the other hand, come to appointments armed with graphs of their child's blood counts, spreadsheets documenting every dose of medicine taken, and spiral notebooks chronicling every bowel movement over the preceding twelve months.

Foreword

Shane Meader was no different. When his then three-year-old daughter Coral was diagnosed with cancer, he educated himself on the scientific origins of her disease, learned how to perform a variety of blood count calculations, then taught himself the biological mechanism of all the chemotherapeutic agents aimed to cure his child. In fact, during the first months of treatment, we would draw diagrams of cancer cell division to illustrate the mechanism of the medicines that would hopefully rid Coral of a potentially fatal disease. When his appetite for knowledge remained unrequited, I recommended texts to him detailing the history of cancer biology, and he read through all of them... twice.

Given the cerebral nature of our personalities and professions, and the fact we have both been known to bring our thumb drives to cocktail parties, Shane and I have been able to forge a unique physician-patient relationship. I had always assumed him to be like every other engineer, until he handed me a document one morning that did not resemble the usual spreadsheet or medication log. I downloaded it to my computer and printed a stack of papers titled "Curing Coral"; a literary account of Coral's medical journey. As I read it that afternoon in my office in Des Moines, Iowa, it reminded me of another afternoon that transformed my view of the science, art, and spirituality of medicine.

Foreword

I recall approaching a church in a small town in East Texas, two and a half hours east of Dallas. The weather is pleasant with almost no humidity; the magnificent part of the year in Texas, just before the onset of the summertime inferno. This church stands as the largest building in this community of a little over two-thousand people; an anachronism of a town that appears more easily accessed by time machine than by highway. A tall, thin man wearing a black cowboy hat and silver belt buckle the size of a saucer waves to me from a distance and motions for me to come over. The Cowboy helps me navigate the crowd outside, equipped with his thick Texas drawl almost incomprehensible to a native New Englander like myself. He escorts me into the church, where I am wearing a navy suit and everyone else is wearing blue jeans. The Cowboy is the father of a patient of mine, and we are at the funeral of a boy who died from complications of leukemia.

Flashback six months before the funeral: I was working at a hospital in Texas at the time, and was in the twelfth of the minimum fourteen years of post-high school education required for me to become a pediatric oncologist. In my first month of training, two new patients arrived around the same time in the late evening. During this evening, I first met the Cowboy, now sitting to my right at the church. His son, a teenager, had arrived with a white blood cell count fifty times that of a healthy child. He was unable to interact with me.

Foreword

His blood, so viscous with leukemia cells, looked like tar as it transferred from his veins to the laboratory vial. These aberrant cells were damaging small blood vessels in his lungs and brain. Even worse, heart failure ensued as he acquired a potentially lethal infection since his white blood cells, though excessive in number, could not function properly to battle bacteria as they would in a healthy child. The Cowboy's son had acute myeloid leukemia (AML), a type of leukemia that carries an ominous prognosis in children. Treatment is aggressive and dangerous. In fact, therapy may be as dangerous as the disease itself. I sat next to the Cowboy, told him the diagnosis of leukemia, and proceeded with discussion balancing realism and hope.

After this morbid conversation, the hour was late. I drank a glass of water and walked down the hall to see my next patient. I was weary, having been awake and working for nearly forty hours. The patient was an eight-year-old boy who was not critically ill, and his blood counts were not abnormal to a dangerous degree like those of the Cowboy's son. We talked about sports and his favorite movies. I then told them that he had leukemia; however, this conversation held more optimism than the one I had with the patient down the hall just moments earlier. He had a different type of leukemia: acute lymphoblastic leukemia (ALL), the most common cancer in children. Given his younger age and only slightly elevated white blood cell count, his prognosis was excellent. Treatment began shortly thereafter, and he went home a few days later. By the end of the first month of treatment, his leukemia could not be detected.

Returning to the funeral; I sat next to the Cowboy again, both of us reflecting in silence. But we are not at the funeral of his son. The teenage young man with the aggressive leukemia and failing organs, the one whose odds were against him, was at school cured of leukemia with all his vital organs recovered. Instead, we are at the services to celebrate the life of the now-deceased eight-year-old boy, the child who should have survived.

The dichotomy could not be more pronounced. In the church in East Texas, this ultimate tragic irony personified the progress of medical science over the past six decades. Not long ago, the workdays of a childhood cancer physician consisted of an endless succession of inevitable tragedies. Today, thanks to the collaborative efforts of physicians, scientists, hospitals, researchers, and patients, the vast majority of children with cancer will be cured. Yet while our treatments and understanding of pediatric cancer have progressed at an unparalleled rate, this moment at the church illustrated our fallibility simultaneously; a striking reminder of the challenges that lie ahead and the suffocating weight of the biological unknown.

Foreword

I looked at the hundreds of people surrounding me, the crowd outside, and the Cowboy. He shook my hand, put his arm on my shoulder, and thanked me. I left after the service and thought of the resonating impact of these boys on their family, friends, and community. Until that day, I did not fully appreciate the layers of complexity that come with a child's diagnosis of cancer. I thought about my profession, and how life's journey brings a young physician from Massachusetts to participate in a Baptist service in rural Texas. That spring day, the artistic, scientific, and spiritual components of the field of pediatric oncology crystallized.

Three years after sitting next to the Cowboy at the funeral, my journey took me to Blank Children's Hospital in central Iowa where I met Shane Meader. While his precocious four year-old daughter with cancer busily directed traffic in the clinic, filled her toy lawnmower with oil, and received chemotherapy, he wrote her story.

It is one told from the point of view of the patient and her family, but unlike other patient accounts of their experience in the medical labyrinth, "Curing Coral" articulates the emotional, spiritual, and scientific aspects of the physician-patient experience with equal clarity. I chose to enter the field of pediatric oncology because I wanted the challenge of masterfully orchestrating these elements; where at one instant I am in the laboratory

Foreword

trying to identify novel defects in DNA which lead to testicular cancer, and later in the same day I will treat the son of a Cowboy who comes into the hospital with a new diagnosis of AML. One half of my brain organizes statistical probabilities, biological variables, and prepares for contingencies, while the other half simultaneously attempts to skillfully manage him and his family through the controlled chaos of the most difficult few days of their lives.

Though my physician colleagues often appreciate this multi-faceted nature of medicine, I have not encountered many patients who could articulate the nature of treating children with cancer as well as Shane Meader. He is one of the few parents whom I have met able to describe the thoughts of both the family *and physician*. His book demonstrates not only his superior grasp of the scientific component of his daughter's disease, but his full understanding of the artistic and spiritual aspects of the field of pediatric oncology as well. As a physician, "Curing Coral" reaffirmed the reasons I chose the profession of pediatric oncologist and I believe parents, patients, and medical providers will undoubtedly benefit from experiencing Coral's journey through the eyes of Shane Meader: engineer, writer, and devoted parent.

I guess engineers aren't all the same.

– Nicholas J. Fustino, M.D., 2013

Preface

This writing is both an outlet for me and a documentary of the situation and events that have so changed our family's lives. As an outlet, it is an expression of the many thoughts, emotions and understandings that have filled me to overflowing. Often I desire to share with others what I've learned. But seeing their blank stares of fading interest as I'm describing how the mechanism of daunorubicin is intercalation of the DNA supercoils during interphase, leading to apoptosis, has curbed my enthusiasm. Also, this writing is a way to organize and solidify these thoughts. As a documentary, I hope it will make permanent the many things that time would erode.

But setting my rather selfish personal reasons aside, I imagine a grander picture, a more noble cause, a giving

Preface

instead of taking. First and most important, my hope is that parents of children newly diagnosed with a disease will find hope and inspiration as they experience the emotional struggles as well as the medical victories alongside us throughout our story in the following pages. Also I hope that "normal" parents enjoy, celebrate, and appreciate thankfulness for that normalcy as they learn the details and nuances of a rare and dangerous disease. And equally important, I hope that health care professionals are able to use this work as a portal to the psyche on the other side of their care. To facilitate all this, I and all those who have helped write and edit this have worked to capture the emotional dynamics and define accurately the physical events.

I suppose a fair warning should be stated here: My worldview is laced throughout this writing. Although it could be offensive to some, I make no apologies for it as there is no separating or ignoring its influence as our lives changed around us. Additionally, there are some fictional passages. They are my attempt to visualize the happenings that I studied but could not witness with my own eyes.

Special thanks to contributing editors Eileen Meader and Mica Meader whose "page turning" of the first draft inspired me to see the project through to completion. Thanks to Craig Stephenson, Shelly Davis, Blossom Baumgartner, Daniel C. Wolfe, and Andy Meader for

Preface

unabashed initial reviews and edits. Thanks to my professional editor David Krause, who inspired the final form and "tightened things up." And separately, thanks to Nicholas J. Fustino, M.D., Pediatric Hematologist-Oncologist, Blank Children's Hospital, who not only patiently, honestly, and clearly answered my many questions, but challenged me when my understandings were wanting or even errant.

Held above all these names, however, are multitudes of children whose names I could never know. These are the children who have gone before us, who have made today's journey passable via the price they paid, which for most was the price of their lives.

Where real names are used in this story, they are used with permission from that person. All other names are fictional in order to respect privacy.

– Shane Meader 2013

Curing Coral

1

FAMILIAR LIFE

Normalcy

Probably just like every American family with the typical 2.1 kids, I had always considered our family of four to be close. Eileen and I were blessed with a healthy son and daughter that played so well together. Mica would hold baby Caden and feed him a bottle, a gleaming smile on her face. She would swing him and bring him toy food. As a toddler Caden was mostly quiet while usually carrying a ball or car or rock in each hand. Mica, on the other hand was, and in fact still is, a singer with a flair for drama, always creating a plot to play with. A couple years later they would get filthy dirty together in the yard, and then pose for pictures. We all had a lot of fun as a happy family of four. But our family number did not remain at four. And, in time, our stock-photo-like life would not last. While I cannot say that we eventually became an unhappy family, we definitely became a changed family.

But this particular time in 2008 was a joyful one. As the hospital room door opened, the kids looked as if it was Christmas morning. In fact, that was only a few days before. They gazed at their new sister, Coral, wide-eyed in joyous awe.

Our nurse looked at Caden. "What do you think?" she asked.

"I was hoping for a brother!" Caden replied, sporting an ear-to-ear grin.

The effect Coral had on our family astounded me. It was completely unexpected. Being concerned about the big kids feeling neglected, Coral's effect was out of phase. She captivated everyone. She drew our already close family even closer than what I imagined possible as we all cared for and loved her. Gradually it became evident that Coral was a blessing to others outside our family as well. And not just the expected new baby intrigue. It went beyond that.

A truth I learned soon after our firstborn was that every set of parents thinks their kids are cuter and more precious than every other. This has always struck me as a bit humorous, yet also as a truth that is no trivial thing.

Normalcy

This truth was reinforced throughout the experience of raising each of our kids. As such, it is nearly impossible to write objectively about Coral.

For what it's worth, her awareness and intelligence put us on notice at ten minutes old. She demonstrated awareness of her hands, rubbing and holding them, and showing more than just passing interest in Eileen's soda. We took advantage of that and started Coral nursing right away!

I don't remember a time that Coral was not making some sort of vocalizations. Her Grandpa Owen once said, "Coral doesn't know how to talk, but that doesn't stop her!" But soon she did know how to talk. And that happened far earlier than either of the older kids, as I remember. Some of that can be credited to her big brother and sister investing so much time in her. Regardless, she had clearly been blessed with advanced communication skills.

Drama has always been a major in our house, with singing as a minor. And expectedly, Coral learned it early on. There were big productions complete with costumes and singing. The big kids rarely played without Coral and often would fight over her. Caden even earned a reputation of hugging her too vigorously. Unfortunately, the result made Coral take a defensive position, sometimes with fists up, whenever Caden would get close.

Eileen first called Coral our self-starter child. A typical scene would go something like this: Coral would want some forbidden item that was out of reach, and so she would ask Mommy to get it for her. And when that didn't work, she would ask Daddy to get it. Then she would ask Mica, and then Caden. After none of us would help her, sometimes even outright denying her, Coral would set out to get it herself, without a complaint. We would catch her in the act using whatever tools she needed to acquire the forbidden object, including chairs and broom handles. Fortunately this impelling disposition endured much, remained unhindered, and assisted her through the coming difficult years.

It must be that all of her characteristics and personalities added up to make Coral a very special treasure to us all. Surely the world revolved around Coral.

Immunity

The human immune system is one of the evidences of God in our world. Such a complex and sophisticated system inside each of us could only be by design and is definitively beyond full understanding. Don't misunderstand that I would dismiss scientific knowledge from the past and present work of so many doctors and researchers. I owe my daughter's life to them. I only express my appreciation and awe of our natural innate and adaptive immune systems, which play such an important role in this story. As such, allow some background on these central characters.

Our immune system begins in the bone marrow, where all blood cell production takes place. Here the immune system's white blood cells, or blood "selves" as Coral calls them, are generated alongside the red blood "selves" and platelets. All of these grow and develop inside the core of our larger bones, transforming from stem cells to so-called blast cells and eventually to their destined form of red cells, white cells, and platelets. They replicate relatively quickly, just as hair cells divide quickly to make the hair on our head grow. Upon maturity these cells leave the bone marrow to flow in the blood stream.

White blood cells come in several varieties, all performing different roles within the immune system. B-cells and T-cells "learn" what organisms to attack through exposure to such entities as a virus in a flu immunization shot. NK cells are able to self-identify tumor cells and destroy them on contact. And Neutrophils subdue and eliminate bacterial infections, for example.

At the basic level, only mature white blood cells are normally found in the blood stream—no blast cells or other immature cells. It is from here as well as other systems of the body that these cells can monitor for foreign invaders, learn of new enemies, and launch attacks within minutes of detecting a threat.

The bloodstream reaches all areas of the body in real time, making the perfect avenue for the immune system to do its work. Alerted neutrophils move through the bloodstream and tissue to find, congregate, and consume bacteria from a cut or scratch. B-cells detect a flu virus, for example, and then recruit T-cells for help in the ensuing battle. Incredibly, both B-cells and T-cells can live on for years as so-called memory cells, like sentinels with heightened awareness for that flu virus.

But blood is far more complex than simply red blood cells and white blood cells. Consider that not only oxygen, but nearly all nutrients are delivered by the bloodstream. Not only does it protect against known and commonly occurring micro-organisms that would do us harm, but also protects against unknown and less likely invasions. Furthermore, as self-preservation, platelets of the blood build a blockade lattice spanning all but the largest breech. These functions and processes performed truly restore meaning to the cliché "life-blood".

Disappointingly, the immune system often goes ignored. Save for the occasional cold or less often the flu, the immune system is not given a thought. As well, this described my ignorant sentiment prior to an immersive education that would soon begin.

Imminent

The weather was atypically warm for a January day in Iowa. We experienced the mild weather while taking Coral to see the doctor for a fever. The pediatrician told us that a virus had been going around with high fever lasting up to a week. She said Coral likely had contracted that virus, and that we should keep the fever down with ibuprofen and acetaminophen, layered if necessary, while the virus ran its course.

The pediatrician was 100 percent correct. The fever would emerge at 103°F between the recommended doses of medication. The virus showed surprising tenacity as we worked against it around the clock for a week. It had an alarming duration even considering the knowledge we'd gained from the doctor.

Did this fever foreshadow the future? Was it physically connected to what would come? These are questions I would entertain in the future. I certainly have more insight now, but they may never be answered with certainty.

The fever did break in early February, and our daily routine returned. We enjoyed about a week of that normalcy.

It was Wednesday evening, February 15, 2012, the day after St. Valentine's Day, that Eileen and I noticed a peculiarity. As we watched Coral play in the living room after supper, we saw that she favored her left leg. It was quite minor as it did not impede her in getting where she wanted to go, even with a bit of running. But seeing a self-starter three-year-old girl with a limp just didn't look right. Wondering if she had bumped her knee or suffered some other injury, we questioned Coral about the limp. She didn't know. It seemed nothing to her.

We had probably forgotten about the limp by the next morning. But it continued. More out of curiosity than concern, we inspected Coral's leg for bruises, but found nothing. We asked Coral if she had any owies. Again, nothing.

By Friday Eileen and I considered that whatever was causing the limp might be getting worse, even though there were still no complaints from Coral. She simply played through it, never talking about it. But Eileen and I were talking about it. We were talking about taking Coral to see her doctor. We decided that with her evidently not in pain and the weekend upon us, we would put it off until Monday. Surely it would turn around and be better by then anyway.

With no improvement yet, by Saturday a sense of concern, even worry, had crept into my conscience. And since worry isn't something I'm normally prone to, I took notice. That night I held Coral's right knee and prayed, and prayed again in the middle of the night. I began to get a bit emotional about it. Something was up. I fought against my fear, my lack of faith that this was just some typical growing pain that would pass soon enough. "It's probably just growing pains," I imagined, trying to convince myself. But there lingered something about the unknown, the source of her continued limp, that I feared. Indeed, there was a major growth force at work. But it would prove a force that was as foreign to me as creative writing to an engineer.

Sunday morning our family scrambled off to church, late as usual. After the first service, as we conversed with friends, they noticed Coral's limp. We all agreed that it looked strange for a spirited three-year-old to have a limp. And I confessed to struggling with worry.

Familiar Life

Our morning church activities continued as I tried to brush off my worry. But alarm soon interrupted the worry.

With Coral gently in tow, her Sunday school teacher found us and said, "She just wants her Mommy."

No longer would Coral walk by herself, even with a limp; she now wanted to be carried. I lifted her into my arms and hugged her tightly. Our anxiety nearing panic, we determined to see our pediatrician first thing Monday morning.

REPLICATION

The complete blood count, or CBC, is a powerful tool for medical professionals and patients as well. It would become a measurement as common to us as a growth chart usually found in children's bedrooms, although, without the color and joy.

The test requires drawing a vial of the patient's blood. The blood is then processed by a sophisticated machine that counts each of the red cells, white cells, and platelets in the blood. The capability of these machines to count large numbers of cells makes for highly accurate results. The numbers, or counts, of each of the different blood cells reveal many different health conditions, some of which might not be seen otherwise.

As an example, significant numbers of immature blood cells can indicate a health problem called leukemia—a cancer of the white blood cells. Leukemia, as with most cancers, is defined by incessant replication. This overproduction presents the most immediate risk as it crowds out healthy blood cells suppressing and eventually stopping their vital functions. In one of its most dangerous forms, leukemia can grow so rapidly as to build pressures in the marrow great enough to cause bones to ache and sometimes fracture.

Patients inflicted with leukemia are at another significant risk: an erroneous diagnosis or lack of diagnosis. This is because outward symptoms—flu-like signs, bone pain, and bruising are a few—are often common and relatively insignificant. Often, by the time a correct diagnosis is made, a patient can have an easily visible serious medical problem. These unreliable outward symptoms make the CBC a vital tool for leukemia diagnosis.

Time is against the undiagnosed leukemia patient. In addition to undermining the blood's normal functions, cancer can get established in separate systems of the body, such as the lymphatic system and the cerebrospinal fluid. Treatment options for the latter are relatively limited because of the natural blood/brain barrier granting the cancerous cells a level of protection. The longer the malignant cells go unchallenged, the greater the chance of robust and therapy-resistant mutations, making treatment more difficult and less effective.

That morning at church we felt fear and urgency. But if a life-threatening clock was ticking, its sound did not reach our ears.

2

OBLIVIOUS JOURNEY

Zero-Day

Monday morning began with our normal routine, except that this morning was pregnant with the looming pediatric appointment. Eileen and Coral took the big kids to school and I went to work. Eileen, Coral, and I were scheduled to meet our pediatrician at 8 a.m.

Dr. Joel was Coral's primary doctor. We have known Dr. Joel for quite some time. He has been our pediatrician for Mica and Caden as well. He saw us shortly after check-in, expertly distracting and capturing Coral's attention with his signature clip-on fuzzy bear as he began the exam. After extensive prodding, pushing, and questioning, Dr. Joel isolated the problem to Coral's right knee. After more investigation, he concluded that he did not know the cause of her knee pain. But he ordered X-rays and a complete blood count to see whether those tests would reveal anything. This may have seemed routine, but would soon prove to be vital.

Eileen and I knew this was not going to be fun, but we underestimated the difficulty of drawing blood from a three-year-old. After a quick sterilizing swab, the tech pushed the thin needle into Coral's arm. No blood. And so began an expedition by needle to find that vein. Coral learned how painful and seemingly malicious a doctor's visit can be.

With enough blood eventually in the vial and Coral's tears waning, the hard-fought sample went to the lab. Eileen and Coral made their way to the X-ray clinic, and I set out for the rest of a usual Monday. At least I assumed it would be.

Mommy and Coral spent the next few hours having X-ray images taken that showed no broken or fractured bones—nothing but normal images. Coral did need some convincing that wearing the heavy "coat" during the X-ray procedure was not such a scary thing, so Mommy wore one too.

Two medical appointments in one morning felt like plenty for one day. But the pediatrician's office called and told Eileen that Coral had been scheduled to see a blood specialist as well. We were to be at the hematology clinic at Blank Children's Hospital in downtown Des Moines early afternoon.

I joined Eileen and Coral for the appointment. Inside the hospital we approached the door that read Pediatric Hematology/Oncology Clinic. I knew what hematology meant, but oncology was a foreign word to me. Regardless, we knew this was the right place. Inside the clinic, a small, brightly painted office area opened to a hallway of exam rooms. The receptionists greeted us and introduced us to Wendy Woods-Swafford, M.D., Pediatric Hematologist-Oncologist, Blank Children's Hospital, lead physician at the clinic.

The next few hours demonstrated the doctor's drive for results and the level of skilled staff and technology at her disposal. While cordial and polite with us and playful with Coral, Dr. Wendy showed an urgency of purpose that was lost on me; I didn't know what was ahead.

Immediately we were sent up to "the floor," Blank Children's Hospital, for another blood draw. As Eileen filled out paperwork, Coral and I made our way through a maze of halls and elevators as though on a journey in a foreign land. We found the right floor and were ushered into a procedure room that housed various medical tools and tool chests neatly arranged around a large table in the middle of the room. Coral was getting wiser about what came next, but the nurses were wiser yet. Their experience showed as they wrapped a screaming, writhing three-year-old in a blanket, pinning her to the large table. The nurse holding her down looked at me as though to ask, "Are you OK? Is this OK?" I nodded approval, realizing that we needed this test, and we needed to get it over with.

Soon they capped off a new vial of blood, secured an IV to Coral's hand, and then let her pick out a toy. As if to exert her independence, Coral chose an orange-and-white foam football over a plethora of cuddly stuffed animals and pretty dolls that filled a corner cabinet. Her choice puzzled us all, but she had earned whatever she wanted.

The toys seemed strange—slightly awkward. This feeling started soon after we arrived at the clinic. Coral was showered with gifts. "What is this?" I wondered. "Entire closets full of toys still in the packaging? Hand-knitted hats...?"

Coral and I returned to the clinic and were then sent for additional X-rays of her leg and knee. And again, the pace felt urgent, even driven. This time Eileen went with us on this new journey through a different maze. The X-rays proved uneventful as Coral posed for "pictures." She may have even had some fun with it. Undoubtedly the morning's X-rays taught her that "pictures" didn't cause any owies. And Mommy was with her just like in the morning. That made it better for sure. And just as the morning's X-rays showed, the black, white, and gray shaded images on the monitor showed normal bones and tissue.

We made our way back to the clinic and returned to the modest waiting room. The day had turned into late afternoon when a nice lady entered, followed by Dr. Woods.

"Would you guys join me in the next room?" Dr. Woods asked casually.

I heard the nice lady ask Coral if she could play with her again. Then she turned to us and assured us that she would watch Coral, that it would be OK. Eileen and I followed Dr. Woods to the next room.

The exam room felt small and confining, almost an invasion of personal space, not unlike the room's intended purpose. Save for the one colorfully painted ceiling tile, the room typified the stark monotone glare of a hospital. Dr. Woods took the rolling stool and Nurse Leslie and Nurse Kelli stepped into the room, closing the door behind them.

Kathy

Throughout the afternoon of zero-day we stayed in the clinic waiting room that doubled as a playroom where Coral found numerous toys to keep her attention. Her toys of choice were play food items, specifically pizza and plates for a pizza party. Fortunately, there were few people occupying the waiting room. I say fortunately because the room was much too small for an actual pizza party.

(The clinic has since relocated to a much-expanded facility on a different floor. It now affords ample space for patients, families, and staff. Hugely generous donations of time and money have created a warm and welcoming reception office, comfortable and effective examination rooms with homey décor, and a dedicated playroom that can actually accommodate a pizza party!

The new space also brought a new and more recognizable name: Blank Children's Cancer and Blood Disorders Center.)

Occasionally, a polite lady would come in to this waiting/playroom and ask Coral if she could play with her. Each time she did this I thought, "How nice," and mentally placed it with the other slightly strange happenings that day.

The polite lady was Kathy O'Connor, Child Life Specialist. Later it occurred to me that Kathy knew our challenge before we did. It was her job. That job, rather, profession, is called Child Life. And its objective is to help kids through the various challenges of being treated at a hospital. This ranges from being at their side for injections to "light saber" duels with glow sticks in a darkened playroom.

The Child Life specialist considers each child's learning capacity while helping the child understand medical procedures. Kids get a sense of peace as they become familiar with a fun person at the hospital, a person that plays with them and stands by them during the painful times. This is one of the noblest of professions, where the salary paid will never equal the value of the services.

Left to ourselves to navigate the emotional and physical trauma of those first few weeks likely would have damaged our family permanently. The Child Life staff did not let that happen; Eric juggled, Melissa talked us through hair loss, Meagan brought painting crafts, Kathy trained Coral about her implanted catheter, and everyone brought toys.

Being unaware that such a profession existed amplified its impact on us and our family. Being unaware of that type of need emphasized the appreciation for those who choose Child Life as a profession.

Kathy is very much Coral's friend now—even reaching the level of "Grandma," although never with that title!

3

ACUTE DESTINY

Personal 9-11

"I'm not one to sugar-coat words or beat around the bush. You can always be straightforward with me."

"Coral has leukemia."

"God is not punishing you."

"She is safe now."

As those few words from Dr. Woods made their way into me, my conscience became a torrent of shock, disbelief, and questioning.

How can she be safe?

How would you know God is not punishing me?

"How reliable is this blood count thing?" I asked, managing to speak out the last question.

"It's *very* reliable," Dr. Woods replied.

As simple and weak as that answer sounded, I felt cornered. The blood count evidence proved nothing to me. But something in me, something that aligned with my prior emotion and fear, knew it to be true. There was nowhere to go but face the reality that Coral Blossom was stricken with a life threatening disease: cancer.

"She would try to fool us," Dr. Woods said of Coral's lack of outward symptoms. All they had to go on was the limp—bone pain. Yet her white blood cell count measured ten times that of a normal child (such a high count placed her in a high risk category), as if to emphasize the diagnosis. Later, Nurse Leslie admitted that upon her first view of Coral, with eyes of experience, even she did not believe Coral would become one of their patients. Only through the deeper studies would proof exist for childhood leukemia.

Dr. Woods, Nurse Leslie, and Nurse Kelli left the little exam room that now held the event of our lives. Things were starting to fall into place in my mind; the toys, the gifts, the hats, the meaning of the word on the clinic door. Eileen looked me in the eye and asked if I was

OK. Unlike every other time she had asked me that question, I slowly shook my head "no" as I choked with tears. She tried to encourage me, "I don't think God gave us Coral just to take her right back."

Armchair Oncology

God wired me as an engineering type. Behavioral tests I've taken reveal me as an analytical and phlegmatic introvert. As such, soon after zero-day I realized that my coping mechanism was going to be learning the why's and how's of treating leukemia in Daddy's littlest girl. I wanted to know—*needed* to know—what we were doing, and why. At the same time I realized that the knowledge and understanding of this disease might be beyond my reach because it was a completely different profession studied for at least a decade by the professionals. As an engineer, I knew and embraced the likelihood that not every treatment (process) would achieve the defined ends (product) at 100 percent, or that every result would be explicable.

Exactly when it was that I started asking questions, I don't recall. But I now have a reputation at the clinic for asking good questions. I think it means that sometimes my questions can be a bit of a challenge, even for the doctors. But I think they appreciate that... at least I hope they do. My research also included online documents. I would pore over them again and again, analyzing, cross-referencing, saving them to my personal flash drive so I could access them anywhere I could find a computer.

In my estimation, the actions of the different chemotherapy meds pointed to an overarching theme of diverse treatment. It seemed the approach was to attack the malignant cells from as many different avenues as possible using as many different mechanisms as possible. But there was also an underlying theme of commonality. The medications are effective because cancer cells replicate quickly. This explains why patients often lose their hair. Their immune systems are hindered, and sometimes they require blood transfusions. Each of these types of cells replicates quickly, making all of them vulnerable to the cancer-killing chemo drugs. (In the back of this book is a list I compiled of chemotherapy medications that directly affected Coral with my interpretation and summary of their action along with commentary by some of our doctors. It is the evidence of my coping mechanism employed.)

The caveat of these medications is the side effects, some of which can be serious. PEG-asparaginase can cause an allergic reaction that can progress to fatal. Vincristine can damage nerves of the extremities, limiting strength, mobility, and dexterity. Daunorubicin and doxorubicin damage not only leukemic cells, but also heart muscle cells that are not easily reproduced. Others yet can adversely affect a younger patient's learning ability. And most of them cause acute nausea. Their effectiveness against cancerous cells is not without a physical price to the patients and an emotional price to loved ones.

Eileen and I learned to respect these drugs throughout Coral's treatment as we witnessed their effects. Some we learned to appreciate while others we learned to loathe. The powerful steroid dexamethasone was our worst enemy because it forced the most awful emotional and physical changes in Coral. But our favorite drug counteracted nausea and it was nothing short of miraculous. Zofran would eliminate Coral's nausea within minutes of ingestion. It would transform her from continuous heaving to peaceful dining in no more than fifteen minutes. We took Zofran with us everywhere. We would have paid the drug's full price, easily more than $100 for a small bottle, out of pocket if necessary.

My supposed degree in armchair oncology has offered practical benefits to Coral's treatment. Medication delivery at home requires competence, commitment, and even a bit of skill. Having some knowledge of why the treatment must be done and how it works helps foster the former. That's not to say we have performed flawlessly, but it has helped us make some good decisions. More than once we've helped nurses access Coral's port (implanted catheter). Despite our sense of feeling apologetic for telling the nurses how to do their jobs, they have always been thankful for our assistance.

One instance in particular I felt that my knowledge was most validated. A significant viral infection had taken hold as Coral's white cell counts approached zero because of dosages of the most powerful medications. We were seeing Dr. Woods to determine whether the next treatment cycle would start or be delayed by a week, which is usually decided by the white cell count of that morning. If it's above the minimum, you continue treatment, and if it's below the minimum, you delay. Leading up to our appointment, I found myself hoping Coral did not meet the minimum counts. My reasoning theorized that her immune system, what little there was of it, could recover enough to help subdue the virus before enduring another crippling round of chemotherapy.

The doctor informed us that Coral would start the next treatment phase that day, provided her blood counts met the minimum requirements. I then sheepishly admitted that I hoped the blood test did not meet counts, and told them of my reasoning. After a few seconds pause and a thoughtful expression, the doctor declared that we would not start the next course that day, regardless of counts.

It is uncertain whether my comment influenced her decision. It is certain, however, that the doctor based her decision on Coral's acute viremia, a viral infection in the bloodstream. Perhaps my reasoning merely happened to correlate with the doctor's opinion, but I took it as confirmation of my armchair oncological assessment.

Along for The Ride

Later that evening on zero-day, with Eileen and Coral settled into their room at Blank Children's Hospital for the upcoming week-long stay, I drove home to prepare for bringing the big kids home. They had been with their grandparents as a result of our normal day run afoul.

It began during the drive. The full burden came to rest as I numbly navigated the now darkened city streets. All outside stimulus faded to scarcely noticeable. Everything paled in comparison to how life had just changed. My conscience told me to prepare to be angry at God because this kind of situation warrants it. Others have admitted such a response to their own personal tragedies.

"Simply expect that it will happen. Who could blame me? After all, how could God have allowed our precious and spirited daughter's life to be threatened?" I protested while on the brink of indignation.

Thankfully, the anger at God never came. What did come were the tears. Maybe it was the grief, so strong that it drowned the smoldering anger as if quenched by a drenching rain. Driving became more difficult. I managed to see through the emotional downpour to stop for the light at University Avenue and MLK Parkway. Later I would joke that just as for texting and driving, sobbing and driving was not recommended. Every waking moment of the next eighteen hours I spent crying for our young daughter's life.

The ride continued the next day—actually for days—back to the hospital as tests, procedures, and surgery happened around us, all the while trying to hold on during this seemingly accelerating ride.

An ultrasound technician performed an extensive study of Coral's heart. Coral took the inconvenience very well while watching a "Backyardagains" DVD. The technician recorded a sort of cryptic home video from several different angles, showing Coral's heart valves opening and closing... blood flowing and stopping... chambers filling and draining. The impressive technology poignantly displayed the significance of this hospital stay.

The itinerary for this day, Tuesday, included surgery to implant a port and a bone marrow aspirate to collect a sample. Both would be done concurrently with Coral anesthetized.

A port can be described as a needle receptacle connected to a catheter, all contained within the patient's body. Nurses can then access the port by inserting a special needle. Simply stated, it makes for easy bloodstream access for blood draw or IV meds, a valuable capability as demonstrated by yesterday's traumatic blood draws. But the planned location of the catheter gave us pause. It would pierce a major vein just upstream of her heart. It was a scary thought: the injection of fluids that would immediately fill our three-year-old daughter's heart.

The bone marrow aspirate would enable a biopsy to detail exact information about the blood factory—the source of leukemia. Extracting bone marrow requires large needles to extract the thick fluid after penetrating the tough outer layer of the bone. We were so thankful they performed this under anesthesia, unlike standard practice of years past.

The hours before that surgery were some of the most memorable. The Child Life staff members were in the driver's seat, distracting Coral before her first major procedure. They decorated paper crowns with purple foam stickers. Laura, the Child Life specialist, peeled off the backing, and then Coral would hastily choose a spot and stick it on the crown. As more and more monitors were connected to Coral, she eventually did not have a free hand to apply stickers. Surprising us all, Coral resorted to pointing with her feet to direct Laura where to apply the next sticker. Laura happily followed Coral's direction. Coral won some new fans as the anesthesia put her to sleep.

4

CELLULAR CAMPAIGN

War

Millions of people deal with cancer every day. Because the treatment is life-threatening, intense, and difficult to cope with, it is labeled a battle or a fight. Slogans like, "I fought cancer and won" are inspired. As the realization of our situation settled, I fully expected to share the same perspective. But all these months later, in my mind at least, the battle analogy never really seemed to fit Coral's treatment. It felt more like a low-level, basic malfunction in her bones that just needed to be reset.

Regardless of my thoughts about Coral's treatment, we learned all too well that treating cancer is a perilous fight. Our many visits to the children's hospital oncology floor mercilessly showed us how serious and dire it can be. I submit that treating cancer is more likened to war than a battle. Like war, treating cancer is often made up of many battles, many treatments. Cancer is not defeated with one battle or one fight. It is an entire campaign.

If we were fighting battles within a war, one of the most fearsome battles we fought occurred during the induction phase of chemotherapy. This is the initial treatment after diagnosis, and includes some of the most powerful medications. The name of our nemesis was dexamethasone. It's a steroid twenty-six times more potent than naturally occurring hormones. This medication commanded an assaulting appetite in Coral. It was a challenge to keep her fed and she constantly complained of hunger while demanding food. One afternoon she climbed down from her chair after eating a full lunch and not so politely demanded supper!

Simultaneously, other chemotherapy medications caused constipation. These opposing forces made a very serious situation that resulted in painful gas and bloating until we found an effective combination of laxative and anti-gas medications.

As if that were not enough, another side effect was nausea. The poor girl was ravenously hungry but sick to her tummy, inevitably vomiting full stomachs.

Tactics

Tuesday's scheduled procedures had gone well. The port had been installed, a bone marrow sample had been obtained, and Coral's vitals were good. Dr. Line, the pediatric sedation specialist, studied Coral's chart as Eileen and I sat waiting for Coral to wake up from the anesthesia. Curious of how we might prepare for this, I asked Dr. Line, "How will she be as she wakes up? Is there anything we can expect?"

After a short pause he reassured us in a comforting voice, "Oh, she'll be fine… she'll be fine."

A bit ambiguous I thought, but I took some comfort from it and sat back in my chair.

Coral woke up angry as a hornet, thrashing about and crying out! And we learned almost every time since that first episode that she wakes up from anesthesia the same way each time. She was fine, just as the doctor had said. Just maybe a different definition of "fine" than I was thinking. I get a good laugh every time I relive that irony. We love and appreciate Dr. Line as much as anyone else at the hospital, and not just to laugh at his expense. It's especially true because his work in the procedure rooms, which is deep sedation of children, is far from a laughing matter.

To this point Coral had been on IV fluids only, save for the anesthesia and maybe some pain medication for the surgery, but no chemotherapy. So it confused me to see the day's CBC showing a reduction in white blood cells. Monday's count was 65,000, with today's count at 49,000.

Dr. Schwalm, the clinic's physician on call that week, assured me that this was normal: "Simply more fluids will flush out some leukemia cells."

I took that as encouragement as we ended our first twenty-four hour day with leukemia.

Wednesday became the first day of Coral's chemotherapy. I probably still thought chemotherapy was nothing more than a different way to deliver radiation, as if patients ingested irradiated pills. I soon learned it was quite different from what I'd imagined.

The previous day's bone marrow study revealed staggering news: 91 percent of Coral's bone marrow was leukemic. On the plus side, the biopsy afforded us exacting tactical information. The study had determined from which white blood cells the leukemic cells originated. The immature lymphocyte blast cells should have matured into B-cell lymphocytes, which are the virus-fighting immune system cells. Instead they stagnated in immaturity, maligned, and were now explosively multiplying. This narrowed the diagnosis from leukemia to Pre B-cell Acute Lymphoblastic Leukemia, or the shortened acronym ALL.

Acting on that information the physicians assigned a "roadmap" of treatment and ordered chemotherapy medications to be delivered immediately. The informal mantra of treating acute leukemia is "Hit it hard, hit it fast." Again, the gravity of our situation surfaced when reading the large biohazard warning emblazoned on the syringe bag; *IV medication: FATAL if given by other routes.*

Meanwhile, the day's CBC white cell count continued its downward trend, from 49,000 to 31,000.

Antagonist

From the view in the bloodstream, the malignant cells' numbers were thinning, likely from the obvious increase in fluids. Everything flowed more freely, now that it had become less crowded. No matter; there were more where those had come from, and there were so many now that replication would sustain the future. These leukemic cells had that advantage. Their unregulated replication cycle could way outpace the healthy cells. Then a new fluid appeared. It seemed to have a red hue.

Within the bone marrow, blood production churned at normal levels. How they could maintain their numbers while dwarfed by the malignant lymphoblast cells was a mystery. Already this growing mass of cells put considerable pressure on the bone. Maybe soon, all resources could be dedicated to the lymphoblasts and end the blood production. Normally, the stem cells would convert to myeloid or lymphoid progenitors, then continue on to the blast cells, further developing into promyelocytes or prolymphocytes, then finally maturing to megakaryocytes or erythrocytes, basophils, neutrophils, eosinophils, monocytes, lymphocytes… so much simpler to replicate the blasts. But what was this new signal? Its message suggested increased production. The message turned to insistence, then to an unrelenting demand. The source was unknown but the effect was welcome.

The occasional NK cell and even a few T-cells resisted the leukemic onslaught by contacting and destroying blast cells. Somehow they were able to identify the blasts, which should have been anonymous cells to them. The result was devastating, sometimes a bit gruesome. The attacking cells lanced their targeted cells, causing them to burst after a short delay. Others simply fell dead. But this was of minor concern. The attacking healthy immune system cells were so few in comparison. Even a coordinated immune response at this point would be meaningless.

Besides, more blast cells were on the way, vastly more, thanks to the demanding signal stimulating the bone marrow, which now felt like a continuous jolt from a lightning bolt. Healthy stem cells and progenitors still multiplied by the thousands, but the malignant blast cells multiplied by the tens and hundreds of thousands. Their numbers overran the marrow and even the bone itself. But curiously, the blasts did not live as long as the normal cells. They were prematurely activating apoptosis, the natural cell death cycle. The mortality rate accelerated and spread through the newly formed cells. Perhaps the intense jolting signal that increased production proved too potent for the leukemic cells to endure. Fortunately, some of them survived and escaped the bone marrow through their favored exit at the lower part of the femur.

The blast cells in the bloodstream continued replicating, which should have been more productive than it seemed to be. Many cleaved and divided, and then did it again. But too many sat idle, probably dead. The massive momentum from a few days ago slowed while the unfamiliar red fluid continued to flow. What was going on?

At a level smaller than cellular, the new fluid's red hue was not as evident. On the molecular scale it became clear that the substance interfered with the DNA replication process within each cell's nucleus. Without a second set of life's blueprints, there was no way to make two independent cells.

The tightly wound DNA chains could be seen relaxing for replication while this alien molecule forced itself between some of the links, and held fast. A unique gene encoded in the DNA and specific to the cause attempted to repair the damage, but repair failed. Other regulatory genes attempted the repair, but the stuck molecule remained. With permanently damaged DNA, replication, both for the DNA and subsequently the whole cell, now became hopeless. There was no alternative; proteins and enzymes would initiate and carry out the death cycle. Unfortunately not only would the cell be lost, but not a single daughter cell could be produced. Worsening matters, this molecule worked not just locally but was also penetrating DNA on a universal scale. It seemed that no cell, leukemic or healthy, could escape the effect of this substance created from some rare red microbe.

Observations

Gradually, throughout Tuesday and Wednesday, the shock and grief subsided enough to allow my situational awareness to rise up. That was also when my appetite for information awakened. Despite understanding very little at this point, observation of the doctors indicated that the bone marrow aspirate contained very important information. They discussed the lab's evaluation of it and the viewing of it under a microscope.

I didn't know that the subject of their complex, obscure words could actually be seen. I wanted to see it. I wanted to see what they were seeing. Maybe it would be beyond my understanding, but I didn't care. I was ready to learn. Admittedly, maybe I held an ulterior motive: seeing proof of leukemia for myself. As it turned out, I saw that it truly was beyond my understanding.

Well after normal hours that Wednesday evening, Carla Schwalm, M.D., Pediatric Hematologist-Oncologist at Blank Children's Hospital, gave me a glimpse into a different world. As I looked through the secondary set of microscope eyepieces, she magnified the image closer three or four times. The image changed from a randomized mass of tiny dots to not quite round purple and bluish circles that filled the view. Most were touching each other while some areas looked really squeezed together. Dr. Schwalm centered some cells in the circular view of the microscope.

"Mostly these are all blasts," she said. "See that one with the four segments in it? That's a seg. And the U-shaped one is a band."

Then I understood. The bands (immature neutrophils) and segs (mature neutrophils) were healthy cells. As the doctor zoomed from area to area of nearly continuous lymphoblasts, I noticed a familiar pinkish-colored, donut-shaped cell—a red blood cell! Something I recognized!

Finally, I asked to see the malignant lymphoblasts. She searched an area and centered it. "See how they are almost entirely nucleus, and how they are misshapen? That is one way to tell. We would have to talk to the pathologist to know for sure."

OBSERVATIONS

Although mesmerized by the microscopic views, I did not fully understand what I saw. I did not realize that while I viewed the slide of Coral's bone marrow under the microscope, the obvious evidence of leukemia stared right back at me through the lenses—lymphoblasts in overwhelming numbers. It would be days later before I understood this. As stated earlier, this out-of-control overpopulation is the hallmark of leukemia.

Divisive

While malignant cells were being lost by the many thousands, still some managed to survive. It might only take one mutation in a single cell out of the millions of leukemia cells to activate a new pathway for survival. That one cell could acquire immunity to the red substance, withstand the marrow signal's potency, and replicate a new wave of momentum. It was unclear if any mutation of immunity ever happened before a new form of cell death ensued, thanks to a little flower.

The little flower was the common ornamental periwinkle garden flower, sometimes called vinca. A chemical refined from it had been employed as a standard chemotherapeutic agent years ago when the flower was discovered to possess a unique destructive biological action.

With the rapid replication cycle of the leukemic cells, mitosis was underway constantly. This was where and when the little flower's chemical applied its destructive effect. As it flowed throughout the bloodstream it permeated through cell membranes and bound to the cell's mitotic structural lines.

Mitosis is a miraculous process that physically creates two identical living cells from one. So many things must happen at the right time and order for mitosis to occur. The DNA, already duplicated by a prior cell process, must strengthen and condense into chromosomes to facilitate and withstand this demanding process. The chromosomes must align in preparation for the physical separation. Structural lines then span the width of the cell to physically pull each identical set of chromosomes to opposite sides of the cell as the cell stretches and splits into two.

Undergoing mitosis, the blast cells' chromosome duplicates pulled apart, beginning their short journey to a new cell only to be left floating helplessly midway as their towing lines severed. Most cells didn't even get that far. The packages of duplicated DNA aligned and awaited the structural lines' attachment that never came. The lines couldn't assemble into lengths long enough to span the cell; they simply disintegrated into worthless fragments. This led most cells to induce the death cycle, the result of gross error in mitosis. Others suffered severe damage to the cytoskeleton, also made of structural lines, and died more acutely. Outer membranes ruptured, cells fell apart.

The anomaly of the marrow, leukemia, was failing. Its DNA was being wrecked. Its cells were being torn apart. And their dead bodies were being flushed away by volumes of fluid. The tide had turned. Leukemic cell death now cascaded exponentially from the unique and awesome actions of the chemotherapy medications known as daunorubicin, dexamethasone, and vincristine. And the near future would bring several more differing medications to further disrupt the malignant cell's reproduction at the cellular and molecular level in just as many differing ways.

The opening battle was over. The war had just begun.

It's Nice to Be Home

And Coral began to feel better. That is, between the chemo effects of nausea and fatigue. She felt so much better, in fact, that Eileen and I found ourselves running through the fourth floor of Blank Children's Hospital dragging "Robot Friend" along, trying to keep up with Coral. Obviously her right knee was no longer hurting. The pressure within her bones was being relieved.

We learned that the IV connection to Coral's port would be continuous during every hospital stay. And this first week we got to know very well the little infusion machine that controlled the IV. It seemed to have a mind of its own as it displayed various messages on its large screen. It also seemed to talk as it summoned the nurses through its audible alarms. The machine effectively became a part of our family when

Coral started referring to it as Robot Friend. The hospital staff caught on as well, and the name stuck.

The five-story building of Blank Children's Hospital proved to be a great place for Coral and many of the other child patients to play, and even included a large playroom on the fifth floor that rivaled many toy stores. But every floor had toys like wagons, push toys and riding toys to scoot around on. Coral came to enjoy pushing a large toy car as fast as her legs could carry her, barely in control while careening off the walls. I wonder if the real fun was actually watching Mommy and Daddy running, fumbling, and detangling Robot Friend!

The CBCs (complete blood counts) on Thursday, Friday, and Saturday confirmed that the downward trend of the blast cells continued its free fall; 12,000, then 5,000, then 3,000. Remission had been induced. This, and likely Coral's generally good vitals and demeanor, meant we might be allowed to go home soon. But it did not mean that the chemotherapy would end soon. The assigned roadmap, or treatment schedule, detailed many treatments that spanned more than two years. Some would be delivered by us at home while other treatments would be performed at our virtual second home, that is, the clinic and hospital. The roadmap scheduled many, many treatments.

It's Nice to Be Home

Dr. Schwalm explained that even considering Coral's rapid progress, the history of such treatments, having been proved by so many kids that had gone before us, showed that unseen or uncounted leukemia cells might still be lingering.

The doctor explained further, "If we leave them alone, they will make a robust comeback. That is why the treatment is so long."

But we did get to go home, and everyone felt the relief.

Coral expressed it best: "It's nice to be home."

Coral and I played in the last snow of the year with Grandma Blossom under a bright and clear sky. I pulled Coral in her sled and Grandma rolled out a snowman while Eileen snapped some photos. Coral was definitely happy to be home, but it was apparent that she did not quite feel her normal self. She was run down, simply worn out by the hospital stay and undoubtedly from the impact of the medications. Later that day she fell asleep at the table while coloring, poor ma'am.

The Knife Edge

There was, and still can be, an intense emotional feeling that would come and go. Eileen and I didn't necessarily feel it at the same time, and it meant different things to each of us.

The days immediately after diagnosis became a disorienting blur of emotions, information, decisions, coordination, and planning. It embodied a paradigm shift of life. Thankfully, Dr. Woods and everyone at the clinic carried us through the next steps after diagnosis, not only for Coral's treatment, but for our whole family's well-being.

Our paradigm shift of life forcibly imposed a much clearer view of what things were truly important. The value of life itself multiplied and intensified. It also revealed an ebb and flow of normal life, and life with ALL. The sum of these things equaled the intense feelings we called the knife edge. It came to be a mutually understood term.

A knife-edge day could be when the sudden realization of Coral's diagnosis interrupts a day of normal routine. The fine emotional balance between the two presents the knife edge.

The treatments that reduced her white blood cell counts to zero felt like living on the edge of a knife. On the one side leukemia threatened, and on the other side loomed any number of quite literally deadly viruses and bacteria. The feeling was that falling off either side would prove fatal.

Call it a fear-versus-faith struggle, although it never seemed that simple.

A Silent Party

The treatments resumed the very next Wednesday at the clinic. Really it seemed an extension of the prior week's hospitalization. The clinic staff checked Coral in, then measured her weight and height along with other vital statistics, such as blood pressure and temperature. Nurse Kelli waited for us in our assigned exam room and enthusiastically greeted Coral. Her agenda was to access Coral's port—to insert the needle that would draw blood for the CBC. I'd like to say that Coral handled it well. But she didn't. The action terrified her.

Coral had a different agenda. "Where's Kathy?" she demanded in deadpan tone.

Receptionist Shelley dialed Kathy's number and put Coral on the phone. "Kathy, where are you?" Coral said. "I want to play."

This scene began to play out every week. One day, after Kathy caught on to the now-routine Wednesday morning phone calls, she surprised Coral. She took the call just down the hall and sneaked up behind her with a "Hi Coral!"

Coral let go of the receiver, dropping it to the floor so she could hug Kathy as Shelley retrieved the receiver by its cord!

These clinic visits became fun, admittedly, probably mostly for the adults. The experience was so positive that I began looking forward to them.

This became the new normal of Wednesdays as our "clinic day," to which Coral learned to ask about almost daily, "What day is it tomorrow? Is it clinic day?" She never warmed up to them. She got quite upset knowing that her port would be accessed, meaning that someone would be coming at her with a needle. It was not painful, but simply scary. Even Coral admitted that it didn't hurt. Kelli became Coral's regular nurse. This was much to the chagrin of Nurse Leslie, who had Wednesdays off and had already requested our clinic day to be changed for that reason!

A Silent Party

The one-month point meant scheduling a pivotal third bone marrow aspirate. A second bone marrow study had already been done on the first of our weekly clinic days, and it did not show any leukemia cells. This was amazingly good news for sure. But this third bone marrow aspirate commanded anxious attention. The success of the treatment program underway hinged upon this exam. Nothing but zero leukemia cells would earn a passing grade.

While the weekly CBC showed no blast cells, the bone marrow study could count the malignant cells at their source. Additionally, this bone marrow sample would be analyzed by a lab in Seattle that had the ability to scrutinize the sample beyond the capability of the local lab. I theorize that it also provided an independent study, thus removing any potential conflict of interest at the local level. Dr. Woods called us with the result: zero leukemia cells. This result awarded Coral the "rapid early responder" designation of the high-risk category, which improved her prognosis.

For perspective, the bone marrow had transformed from 91 percent leukemia cells a month ago to not a single leukemia cell now counted.

There were no balloons, no cake, no noisemakers, no singing. Our family had a silent party. We praised God for his work in Coral. I had a deep desire to share the news with all the doctors at the clinic, even though they probably already knew. I wanted to celebrate the incredible news with them. I was, still am, so thankful for their work. I had so much joy that I didn't know what to do with it. It might have been at that point that I began to genuinely believe, even expect, that Coral would be OK, that she would survive.

5

INEVITABLE RESULTS

Reject

My relational perspective of our doctors, nurses, and staff has taken on a different dimension of treatment than you might expect. Having quite literally saved Coral's life, they've become superheroes to me. Yet they probably feel like they are just doing their day-to-day jobs. In light of this contrast, I have had difficulty finding the correct and appropriate way to relate to them, which has caused some awkward moments.

One of Coral's enthusiastic nurses, I'll just call her Stephanie, was engaged in caring for Coral and playing with her. She proved so capable, so impressively comforting and entertaining with Coral. And I'd witnessed her treating other kids at the hospital the same way. So impressed with her ability and enthusiasm, and myself almost feeling a part of the team at this point, that I presented my fist to her for a fist bump as if to say, "good job, awesome work..." and she did not respond. I waited another second... no response. Then she gave Coral a fist bump.

OK, what just happened? I quickly dismissed the incident. But later, the more I thought about it, the more it upset me. Was my intent completely misunderstood? What could she have thought I meant? As I imagined some of the possibilities, the implications horrified me.

It was an error in judgment by me. It taught me to check my emotions and thoughts before interacting with staff. It became a continuous check and double check so I would not cause any more awkward moments, or worse. There were some great successes of showing our appreciation appropriately, but there were still some failures as well. It became an unforeseen and unwelcome battle in my own mind.

The Blood Line

In the second month while studying the roadmap, I noticed a medication delivery labeled IV or IM (intravenous or intramuscular) scheduled between our Wednesday clinic days. It appeared that it was to be delivered at home. The implications of the IV and IM took a while to sink in...

"That must be a mistake," I muttered.

Or maybe they intended Coral to come in for this particular medication delivery. All medication given outside of the hospital or clinic to this point had been oral. I made it a point to ask about this during our next clinic visit.

Inevitable Results

A casual question to Nurse Kelli confirmed, "Yes, is that OK? You can do it," she said, as if to instill some confidence in us for delivering IV/IM medicine at home.

But it felt like Eileen and I were left with two impossible choices. We could choose to perform a needle injection or port delivery. Adding to our apprehension, the roadmap required the medication be given four days in a row. Neither Eileen nor I had any medical training. How could they trust people like us to deliver very serious medications by very serious methods? All I could think of was the port line leading almost directly to Coral's heart.

"Wasn't the risk too great? They are asking too much," I thought.

Kelli assured us that they would help us and teach us to do it. She said if we were still uncomfortable, a home health nurse could be employed.

We decided to deliver by IV, by port. It would avoid the pain of a needle into Coral's leg. Pushing a syringe of medication into her port, which would already be accessed from the week's clinic visit, would cause no pain at all. And she was familiar with receiving medication in her "tubies," which was Coral's name for the IV tubes connected to her port. But I continued to waver in apprehension. The responsibility and risk felt as if we had been asked to pilot an airplane with passengers. Lives were at stake here. Nurse Leslie walked us through the procedure and wrote step-by-step the delivery process for cytarabine, also known as ARA-C, by port access.

Later that evening, psyched up and mentally focused, I shut out all distractions as I detailed each step and gathered the correct syringes and tools. Eileen settled Coral in front of her favorite television program during the procedure. I stretched the nitrile gloves onto my hands, sterilized the port tube tip, flushed the line, pushed the ARA-C, flushed the line again, and pushed the heparin syringe to finish the procedure. It was all over in a few minutes, with no tears.

But I felt my own blood leaving my head when Eileen called down from Coral's room the next morning, "There's blood in the line!"

That meant blood had flowed back through the port, through the needle and into the external tubes. The tubes should be clear of blood and filled with the transparent anticoagulant heparin.

Two questions rang out in my head as I rushed upstairs to Corals' room. "Is she OK?! What had I done?!"

INEVITABLE RESULTS

The crimson-traced tubes connected to her port stood out boldly as they draped over Coral's tender skin. She was sitting upright in bed, alert but calm. Apparently she felt fine. Now for the next panic: Had platelets coagulated and plugged the line?! Then I saw the problem. I had forgotten to clamp off the external tubes. What a colossal error. Surely I had ruined the port by allowing blood to clog it. Who knows what surgery would have to be performed to fix it. Thankfully, the external tube's built-in check valve prevented an open flow from the port, which as an end I did not care to imagine. With urgency I ran back downstairs and prepared a syringe of saline and a syringe of heparin while getting sterilized with gloves and alcohol wipes. Returning, I attempted to push the saline... it went with ease... now the heparin... and CLAMP THE TUBE.

The line was *not* plugged—it was functioning normally. The wave of relief felt refreshing, but I was driven to prevent that type of error from happening again. My solution was to print and laminate Nurse Leslie's list so I couldn't *possibly* miss a step the next time. The step-by-step instructions on a large laminated sheet gave me unmistakable guidance and a platform to work from for the various tools. It even allowed me to check off each step with a dry erase marker as I completed them.

So when the very next morning Eileen called down from Coral's room, "There's blood in the line again," this time I was angry.

"*How in the world* could this happen again?! I am incompetent! It's obvious someone else should be doing this," I chastised myself.

After calming down a bit, I noticed that I had indeed engaged the tube clamp. But I had clamped it up against the hard plastic fitting. That prevented the soft tube from pinching shut.

With the same urgency as the first time, I prepared a syringe of saline and a syringe of heparin while getting sterilized with gloves and alcohol wipes. Would I be so fortunate as to easily clear the line, just as I had the first time? I attempted to push the saline… it went easily… and the heparin… and clamp the tube—IN THE RIGHT PLACE.

Now my motivation was to perform the remaining port deliveries flawlessly, as opposed to finding new ways to screw it up. They did go flawlessly, and I felt a bit of redemption along with a regained sense of competency.

Pirates Don't Take Bactrim

Treatment of this form of leukemia, or ALL, includes many deliveries of medication by mouth, sometimes several times a day. Before diagnosis Coral would take the occasional children's medicine at home with no problem. To this day she will willingly take all of her medicines, even though it may take quite a bit of convincing beforehand. But there was a period when it was not so easy.

During the first hospital stay, as the meds and their frequency mounted, she resisted. Eileen and I, taking suggestions from the nurses, exhausted many of the so-called tricks, such as hiding the medicine in chocolate pudding and ice cream. Alas, Coral detected the medications, and even today those desserts are now ruined.

Inevitable Results

One particular time in the hospital, Coral reached her limit when Nurse Emily handed her half of a pill and asked her to swallow it. With impressive form, Coral pitched that half pill across the room, leaving me with my jaw dropped open in astonishment. Eileen and I apologized over and over and directed Coral to apologize too.

Nurse Emily couldn't have been more calm or cool when she responded, "That's OK. I have the other half."

Coral displayed other entertaining and creative ways to resist swallowing her meds, particularly at home. In one instance we found her standing with a clothes basket over her head, a sort of medication guard. Very creative, I thought.

A different time, as Eileen brought Coral her meds while she played in the living room, she simply stated as matter-of-fact, "Pirates don't take Bactrim." Apparently she was playing pirates.

And the least tasteful antic, to which we had to bite our lips to keep from laughing, was when Coral stuck out her bottom and said, "Give it to my bum."

But we couldn't completely hide our laughter, and Coral caught on to it. Then it became something like a nasty rap video.

"Give it to my bum, bum, bum. Give it to my bum, bum, bum," Coral chanted, all the while waggling her bottom in our direction, followed by devious giggles, the little bugger!

Sadly, taking meds rarely involved laughter. More often it produced tears. One day in particular, Coral had a revelation concerning her medication. In a puddle of tears she asked, "Why do you guys give me the medicine that makes me have a bad day?"

Coral had figured out that the steroid prednisone, "PRED-knee-zone" pronounced by her, caused the mood swings that transformed her from joyous play to puddles of tears in a matter of minutes. Her question made Eileen, Grandma Blossom (we were visiting Grandma at the time), and I feel horrible, and it made us cry too. We simply told her that the medicine keeps her out of the hospital. She accepted that answer.

In addition to medication by mouth, Coral received regularly scheduled chemotherapy delivered directly to her spinal fluid. The chemo delivery procedure appeared relatively easy despite involving a long needle inserted into her lower back. Perhaps the facilitating sedation proved a more risky operation. Eileen and I never really had a problem with the sedation. We understood it to be quite a serious procedure, but so was our entire mission. Even if it would have been allowed, the alternative of lumbar puncture with Coral fully awake certainly did not appeal to us.

Coral never really had a problem with sedation either, except for waking up from it quite cranky. Kathy was nearly always with Coral as she fell asleep. Usually Kathy would console her about going to sleep.

"Coral, it's OK to feel sleepy," Kathy told her once.

"Is it ok to feel dizzy?" Coral replied.

Her response was followed by "Aww" all around the room from the doctors, nurses, and technicians present for the procedure. Kathy assured Coral that dizzy was OK, and I held her a little bit tighter before she fell asleep.

On a different day, while Coral worked on a craft, Kathy told her, "Coral, it's time to go see the sleepy medicine doctor."

Disappointed to leave her craft, Coral responded begrudgingly, "I've seen a lot of sleepy medicine doctors in my day."

Pirates Don't Take Bactrim

What a true statement! Her undeniable truth nearly drew applause from the clinic's full waiting room.

Defenseless

Through the third, fourth, and fifth months we continued to adjust to our new life of continual medications and weekly clinic visits while also experiencing hair loss and blood transfusions as well as many other previously mentioned side effects of chemotherapy.

That first night in the hospital, Child Life specialist Melissa talked with each of us about the fact that Coral was going to lose her youthful, silky blonde hair that she had worked on for three years. Coral's hair was slow to come in as an infant. And Melissa noted that the hair loss would emotionally affect us more than it would Coral. She pressed us about how we felt about that. We may have offered opinions, but we didn't know. The feelings that came later could only be experienced.

Coral did not want us to cut her hair. She screamed whenever we suggested it. Eventually it had to be done. We do regret not cutting her hair sooner. It became patchy and thin—an image that we could have spared her. Additionally, she had to wear a hat in direct sunlight. Eileen decided that since Coral had no choice in this matter, the least we could do is let her decide whether to wear a hat at any other time. I felt a bit concerned about keeping her hat on in public. Eileen didn't care a bit what others may have thought. This was her precious daughter. She wanted her to have the freedom to choose when she had no choice in so many other matters. And Coral removed her hats often. They became uncomfortable.

During bath time one evening, Coral's hair loss hit us the hardest. As Eileen washed Coral's hair, the thinning appeared much more pronounced as she wetted it. Eileen became overcome with emotion. It was a harsh reminder of Coral's diagnosis by way of physical proof. This is when Eileen reached out to her online knitting group. Knitters need no excuse to knit, and this proved to be a worthy cause; hats for Coral and moral support for Eileen. We welcomed both and were very thankful.

Coral became accustomed to her baldness, likely because of seeing other kids in treatment. And Child Life provided dolls that were correct for the situation; dolls with no hair or with removable hair. Later we found Coral removing the hair from all of her own dolls and figures that she played with at home. After all, that was correct, that was normal. More recently her hair has somewhat grown back. She sees her bald head in photos from the past and comments, "I hate that." I'm not sure if it is the image itself or the reminder of unpleasant experiences at the hospital.

The few blood transfusions we experienced proved to be an easy process. It felt little different from receiving many of the IV fluids as we had before. And thankfully Coral had no allergic reactions, which was a real possibility. The one traumatic experience happened in the evening after a transfusion. Coral tripped and fell on the hardwood floor of our home. For unknown reasons she was unable to catch herself, and she hit her mouth hard. Instantly her front teeth bled and she cried painful tears. We picked her up and tended to her emotions and injury when I had a dark-humor thought; "No! We just got that blood!"

It was in the sixth and seventh months when Eileen and I had looked back a few times and considered that Coral had not gotten any fevers or sickness since diagnosis. A compromised immune system commonly results in viral infections and is an expected occurrence for leukemia patients in treatment. We knew that any fever would mean an instant trip to the ER. Those with experience in this had warned and prepared us for those "extra" hospital visits. Curiously, that had not happened to us even though three or four such incidents would have been common by now.

Our family had become good at hand-washing, and we were all vigilant of any potential viral and bacterial intrusions. To improve our odds, and per doctor's orders, we stayed away from our relative's farm, one of our favorite getaways. Not that our favorite farm somehow incubated production levels of the most dangerous viruses and bacteria, but it was simply an unknown best left out of our equation. But even the most thorough practices could not prevent every possibility of infection. Especially during the final intense treatment phase that had reduced Coral's immune system to nothing.

"What is that?" Eileen asked. It began as a few small marks on Coral's ankle and lower back.

"Hmm, I don't know," I replied, refusing to say out loud what I thought it was, as Coral had been playing outside in the back yard with friends lately. "We'll keep an eye on it."

Clinic day was only a few days away, so we took comfort in knowing the doctors would soon see what had concerned us. Dr. Schwalm did see the lesions on Wednesday and agreed that it looked like poison ivy.

The rest of clinic day played out as normal, and we returned home after the chemotherapy procedures.

Sleeping problems had already been a recurring issue, so when Coral woke up that night complaining of leg pain, it did not seem much out of the ordinary. A bit of children's Tylenol sufficiently calmed her. Thinking the lesions were poison ivy, we asked Coral if they itched and gave her Benadryl.

But her continued pain ushered us back to the clinic late the next day, especially since pain in the very same leg had begun this entire journey. Nearly everyone was a bit surprised to see us the day after our normal clinic day.

As the elevator doors opened to the clinic's floor, there stood Kathy. She looked more surprised to see us than we were to see her!

Her eyes widened and after hesitation she said, "Well, hi Coral!"

Then she gave Eileen and me a guarded, questioning look, as if to say, "What are *you guys* doing here?"

Eileen said almost apologetically, "We're having some pain. So we came to see Dr. Schwalm."

Inevitable Results

True to their form, the clinic staff handled Coral's newfound pain and our concern seriously and with great interest. They got right to work. Dr. Schwalm examined the marks. Nurse Mary examined them too. Nurse Mary suggested that it could be shingles. To be sure, they swabbed a sample from one of the lesions for lab analysis. The results would take a few days.

More immediately, Dr. Schwalm set out to do some additional research, and she ordered a magnetic resonance image (MRI) of Coral's leg to see what could be causing the pain.

Dr. Nick stepped in a bit later and recommended that we also take a bone marrow sample during her sedation for the MRI (patients must be motionless while the imaging is performed, thus the reason for sedation). Dr. Nick is Nicholas J. Fustino, M.D., the physician who fielded the majority of my questions throughout Coral's treatment. His suggestion for the bone marrow sample was to confirm that the source of the pain was not a resurgence of leukemia cells, "Just to make us all feel better," as Dr. Nick put it. Eileen and I wholly agreed with that idea. They scheduled the MRI and bone marrow aspirate for the next day.

Grandma Blossom joined us for the procedures, which took us down into the quiet and dimly lit surgical facilities of the hospital's lower levels. A few tense hours later we all breathed a sigh of relief when the MRI showed nothing out of the ordinary and the bone marrow showed no leukemia cells. We were still left with no diagnosis of the pain, but at least no greater threat like a relapse of leukemia or bone cancer had occurred.

Later, Dr. Schwalm would confirm by the locations of the lesions that, indeed, it was shingles. And the source of the virus, as if a dose of cruel irony, was a chicken pox vaccine (a live virus type of vaccine) from two years before now unleashed by a lack of immune cells to keep it at bay.

Give My Pants a Rest

Eileen and I maintain that Coral's formidable will had kept her in disposable pull-on diapers. There was no doubt that she knew when she had to go, and she had experience of being on the toilet. Nevertheless, she would hide in the living room to do her business. More disturbing was her outright lying about it. Naturally, the weeks and months after diagnosis put the completion of potty training way out of our sight. But later, several three-day hospital stays for high dose chemotherapy put it back on our agenda.

At the hospital the nurses kept track of everything Coral did, which included everything that came out of her. In fact, her urine was an important measure, which was used to monitor the level of the chemotherapy medication called methotrexate in her system. The analysis called for collecting samples from her full diapers—diapers full of toxic chemo meds, that is. Watching the nurses tediously and cautiously press and wring the urine samples out of gauze from her diapers prompted us to set a goal. For the last hospital stay of this phase, we wanted Coral to be potty trained.

It made me a little nervous when Eileen told Coral she could have anything she wanted for keeping her pants dry and using the potty. With no hesitation Coral declared she wanted a soccer goal. She had been kicking a ball with her friend David, also a three-year-old patient with the same diagnosis, in the hallways of the hospital's fourth floor. They were pretty good at it. I wondered just how much this soccer goal would cost. And one cannot have a goal without a ball!

Eileen and I, mostly Eileen, worked diligently with Coral and she did it. She wore big girl pants for the last high-dose chemotherapy treatment. The nurses were able to collect samples from the toilet-fitted container. Sure, she had some accidents. And she still wore diapers at night. But she had achieved her potty goal and the soccer goal. She chose a shiny pinkish-purple ball to go with it. The price rang up very reasonably, much to Daddy's relief.

Disappointingly, shingles put an end to the success. It could have been the pain, or the medication, or the hospital stay, or all three. The whole experience was just too much for Coral to maintain control of her potty responsibilities. And the whole shingles experience was too much for us to demand it of her. We went backwards. She went back to pull-on diapers all the time, never told us when she had to go, and even lied about it when asked.

After the shingles experience Eileen and I worked on her about potty training. Probably not as consistently as we should have, but we pressed her hard to tell us when she had to go, and put her on the toilet even with her protesting.

Her exasperation with it showed through one day when she demanded, "Give my pants a rest."

As we have known for well over a year, Coral's personality and tenacity make this a decision that is hers alone. She knows that "pretty school" (preschool) this fall will not allow diapers. I'm sure her excitement of going to school will be the final motivation she needs.

Consequences

Within a few days the shingles virus multiplied and spread. More and more lesions appeared, eventually covering half of Coral's right leg, only a few more on her back. And gradually, the frequency and severity of the pain increased. The crying out in the middle of the night became beyond the ordinary. Eileen and I cast aside my normal reluctance to give her oxycodone (I was concerned about addiction to the powerful pain relief medication) and we gave it regularly, which afforded all of us a few hours of relief and peace.

Unhindered, the viral pain steadily continued its ramp-up and soon overpowered the relief of the oxycodone doses. Relief lasted only about an hour. Eileen called the clinic to ask about our dosage options; how much, how often. They allowed us to increase the dosages and we did so right away. I don't remember how much the increased dosages helped, but it was not enough. The torturous waves of pain made Coral scream out from peaceful sleep every night. Clinic day couldn't come soon enough.

Shingles is the disease herpes zoster, which is caused by the virus varicella zoster. This is the same virus that causes chicken pox but by a different avenue. Chicken pox can cause lesions over any and every part of the body. Shingles is a virus that infects the nervous system, which causes lesions at the specific location where the nerves reach the skin surface. This is how Dr. Schwalm confirmed the diagnosis, by those locations. Zoster infecting the nervous system causes waves of sharp, intense pain as well as irritation and itching, like chicken pox. We were learning all about the pain.

Soon after our arrival at clinic, the staff realized how much the disease had spread. And then they quarantined us. The airborne-capable virus was very contagious. Put that in a clinic full of kids with compromised immune systems and the implications were particularly bad. The doctors, nurses, technicians, and even Kathy completed our normal clinic day activities by donning masks and gowns in addition to the normal gloves and sanitizers.

That clinic day turned into our first "extra" hospital stay. Nurse Kelli checked us into a special infectious disease hospital room on the fourth floor of Blank Children's Hospital. The otherwise normal hospital room possessed a curious technology of negative atmospheric pressure. The heating/cooling system continuously drew air into the room and exhausted it outdoors, preventing the room's air from flowing to the rest of the fourth floor and spreading the disease. I thought it was a brilliant new innovative design. It turns out that the concept was not new at all, but actually decades old.

This interesting room and system made for a regular comical display. The technology required the door to be shut for the system to work properly. Apparently it was not used often, because nearly all the nurses left the door open, even if only a crack, while performing their various duties. This set off the negative pressure alarm. Some had no idea what the alarm meant, and so they never got used to it. We constantly shut the door to quiet the alarm. It was such a common occurrence that it became a bit humorous to us as well as the staff.

The proliferation of the disease made it clear that Coral's severely compromised immune system needed help to defeat this virus. But immediately she needed relief from the pain. That became the first priority. Surprisingly, finding an effective medication and dosage did not come easily. Relief came slowly and methodically. Eventually some resemblance of rest returned, both for Coral and Mommy. In reality, the additional rest still did not quench their exhaustion. But the improvement was much appreciated.

Next came the battle against the varicella virus. Dr. Nick, being on call at the time, informed us that he consulted an infectious disease doctor who would be visiting us and directing the treatment. The doctor prescribed a medication that I later learned to be as advanced and high tech as the chemotherapy meds we had learned so much about. Its name was Acyclovir, and it, too, directly disrupted DNA to prevent replication—in this case, replication of the varicella virus, not cancer cells as for the chemo meds. Coral hated the taste. She learned it by name because of that.

"Medicine?! Acyclovir?! NO! NO! NO!" she would yell.

Taking it four times a day made it all that much worse. Thankfully, she took it, and thankfully, it drove back the virus. Although not as quickly as we'd have liked it to. She had to take the medication continuously for four weeks. In time, the pain was gone, but only very slowly did the lesions fade. Day to day, there seemed to be no change. Even today at six months later, the lesions can still be seen very faintly.

Eleven days later we were discharged from that hospital stay. More accurately, Coral and Eileen were discharged. I'm sure Eileen would have other descriptive words than "hospital stay" since she stayed with Coral the entire exhausting duration.

6

Guarded Victories

Attitude

Sometimes during our hospital visits, we could not help but notice a difference in how others handled their own situations. So what has been the difference with the way we've handled cancer treatment compared to others at the hospital?

There was no conscious decision on our part to accept this fate, embrace the treatment, or remain positive. But frequent comments from various staff members, like "You guys look great!" and "You guys are doing so well" made us feel like we were doing something right.

I suppose it was that first day when we either consciously or subconsciously decided to make the best of what we couldn't change. Honestly, it is probably more a matter of who we are instead of some plan to endure a hardship.

We have hope in life. We are firm believers that God helps his people through trials. The Bible records far more events of God giving people hope through trouble than delivering them from trouble. Imagine Noah's hope for dry land amidst unending seas. Consider Jairus' hope that Jesus could heal his daughter who had already passed.

A few inspirational sayings that seem to capture the attitude:

When you get disappointed you have to get reappointed. – Joyce Meyer

Get busy livin' or get busy dyin.' – Andy Dufresne, Shawshank Redemption

You don't know how strong you can be until you have to. – Blank Children's Hospital patient's T-shirt

Admittedly, this attitude was the furthest thing from my mind upon diagnosis. In fact, I probably outright rejected it at the time. The shock and grief were just too much to allow a strong and hopeful attitude. This perspective is not something that can be demanded. It must come from within a person, and it is difficult to

Attitude

do. Willing yourself to have a good attitude is impossible. I have no illusion of being qualified to give advice on the subject.

What I do know is that attitude makes a difference. Struggling and fighting against a disease and treatment arguably undermines treatment, and definitely makes for a miserable experience. I fully realize that this is easy for me to say as Coral has had a great prognosis. She is going to survive, and she is doing very well. So in our circumstances, a good attitude has come easily. But I have no grounds to accuse others for whom the outlook isn't so promising.

On a lighter note, a strange quirk borne of this attitude found me dressing a bit more "decently" for clinic visits. Early on, I inexplicably felt compelled to dress professionally for clinic day. Maybe this was my way of showing professional respect for the clinic doctors and staff. Others dressed much more comfortably, wearing T-shirts, shorts, sweats, and flip-flops. I looked a little out of place at the clinic!

Press

By this time, Coral's vibrant personality had become quite well known throughout the hospital, not just at the clinic. Dr. Nick's word for her character was "direct." I believe the word formulated in the first thirty seconds of his first exam. I don't remember for sure, but Coral was probably telling Dr. Nick to share his stethoscope with her, or that she wanted his otoscope to check his ears when he stated, "She's very direct," with a taken aback expression.

Additionally, we covertly learned that Dr. Nick had later given Coral the nickname "veloci-Meader," referring to her vigor and directness. And she didn't reserve this personality for just a few favorite staffers. Anyone within earshot was a potential target. Most who met

Coral did not forget her. This popularity probably facilitated the TV interview.

Early in November, Kathy asked Eileen and me if we would consider being featured by KCCI channel 8, the local TV news station, for the annual Blank Children's Hospital and Child Life fund-raiser called Festival of Trees and Lights. Coral's story had already been covered on Child Life's annual mailing flyer the past summer, so that made us feel a bit more comfortable with the TV idea. It was still quite a scary thought being on TV. But Eileen and I felt strongly about helping Child Life raise awareness for their cause and money for their budget. We decided that we should do it because we had benefitted directly from both their cause and their budget.

We all determined that Child Life's playroom would be the best place to record the interview. Coral would be most comfortable there, it provided a great background, and it afforded plenty of room for the several people involved in this undertaking. To our relief, Coral had a great day and showed the full effect of her vibrancy and directness!

"Hi Kathy! What did you do to your hair?"

"Kathy, I'm going to be on TV."

Press

Replacing the dipstick on a toy mower, "No more oil!"

The experience was a great success. Much of it had to do with the exceptional editing by the cameraman/editor as I felt my own interview sounded terrible. He made us all look and sound quite good, and he expertly captured Coral's charm and vigor! Coral quickly captured anchorwoman Cynthia Fodor's heart, and it came through on the finished video.

Later, during the festival itself, they put Coral on live TV after airing the prerecorded interview.

In front of the eye of the live camera, Cynthia asked Coral, "Did you tell Santa what you want for Christmas?"

Coral turned her attention from the many distractions of the festival to address her, "Yeah, a cookie. A Christmas cookie!"

Most important, the ultimate and final measure of success was the record amount of dollars raised and the record attendance for the 2012 Festival of Trees and Lights. We trust that we contributed to the success of the fund-raiser, even if only through the small part we played.

Spiritual Matters

Throughout the whole experience, there existed a spiritual dimension that I haven't yet elaborated on. Right or wrong, the spiritual aspect was not driven by me. I was working out my own faith among the other pressing matters. Nonetheless, an outpouring of prayers came forth. Reports of prayers for Coral poured in somewhat expectedly from our church family, unexpectedly from strangers. The magnitude of prayers felt overwhelming. Eileen and I could not fathom the support we were receiving.

Considering Coral's fragile immune system, we could not take her to church for prayer, especially by so many people. Still, I wanted to honor, respect, and show appreciation for all these prayers. I had an idea that led me to take action. It seemed Biblically sound.

I placed my hands on Coral. I put one hand on her upper leg, over her femur, the largest bone in her body, and also the largest reservoir of blood-making marrow. I placed my other hand on her lower back and hip, over the vulnerable cerebrospinal fluid, and another large bone. I then asked God if he could direct the prayers of so many through my hands to where Coral needed it most. Could I place my hands on Coral in the place of all these people praying for her? I didn't know, but I did it anyway. I did it daily for months. In similar fashion, I prayed over Coral's heart after doses of doxorubicin and for the previous doses of daunorubicin. These were the medications that had a reputation for damaging the heart.

God made each of us with talents and abilities. Whether we cultivate these by guidance from him as a believer may mean the difference between excellence and mediocrity. But this is not my point. I believe that just as I experience the uniqueness of my talents, physicians and researchers surely possess the same. My experience is that my talents that seem ordinary and natural to me can be foreign, even impossible to others. To me this stark dichotomy explains that our talents are from God, and not created by man.

To say that God healed Coral is 100 percent true. More specifically, it was done through the minds, hands and spirits of physicians, researchers, nurses, technicians, and so many others using God-given talents for this cause. Just as the Bible is full of records of God working through people, he worked through Coral's treatment team as well.

It was God alone, however, who made Coral strong. Even with 91 percent of her bone marrow leukemic, Coral's body was still able to produce normal numbers of matured healthy blood cells. Or maybe the timing was early enough that the lymphoblasts had not yet crowded out the healthy cells. In either case, the strong amount of good cells was not something any of us were in control of. Coral also took some of the medications in stride, seemingly unaffected by them and not showing typical side effects. Some people commented that "Coral is a tough girl." Or "Coral is a fighter." At the time, I dismissed this as just a polite saying. But in time I came to believe it; God made Coral strong.

Maintaining

These recent days Coral is in the treatment phase called maintenance. The title, which is documented on the treatment roadmap, seems to refer to its goal of maintaining the white blood cell count at a low level. But it also inadvertently foreshadowed the "fixing" or "repairing" implication of the word.

Early in this phase the doctors recommended that we have Coral evaluated for physical therapy treatment. To my eyes she looked like a normal four-year-old girl that could run and jump and play like any other child. I'm so glad the evaluation was not left up to me. To Karen, who would be our therapist, Coral's deficiencies were obvious. She did not pick up her feet when walking, and her right leg appeared noticeably weaker than the left, to name just a few of the problems. These muscle and nerve weaknesses were likely effects of chemotherapy and the shingles disease.

Coral actually enjoyed going to weekly physical therapy sessions. Eileen and I are quite proud of her performance, for which she even earned a trophy at the completion. The sessions included many different creative play exercises designed to work the deficient muscles. They were also designed for fun in order to draw young children. That was the key to Coral's engagement. But Karen had to work on her as well. The exercises were genuinely challenging. While Coral would often want to give up, Karen relentlessly coaxed her on to complete each challenge. Coral emerged from the training stronger than ever, dancing and tumbling with vigor and joy.

The maintenance phase of chemotherapy is much less intense compared to the prior phases, so much so that it almost feels as if treatment has ended. The feeling is relative as we still give Coral different chemo meds daily, weekly, and monthly. The real difference is that we now visit the clinic monthly instead of weekly.

Obviously, the reduced frequency and pressure of the maintenance phase is good. But this became yet another difficult adjustment for me. I found myself longing for interaction with the clinic and hospital staff and blood count data more often than monthly.

Maintaining

In the Preface I stated that this writing began as an outlet. It filled a void as well. The routine of weekly clinic visits lasting at least four hours each, as well as several hospital admissions over eight continuous months, had solidly cast our new normal. Relationships had been forged beyond simply chatting about the weather. I was learning about ALL (the form of leukemia Coral had), and Coral was being cared for. Our "team" gathered data and applied it to what was unequivocally the most important project I'd ever been a part of.

Then it ended as if a switch were flicked off. The next week came and our normal clinic day... was no longer. Coral didn't mind a bit that she could now avoid the port access. That needle terrified her. But I began to feel a deep void. We did not greet Nurse Kelli or discuss immunology with Dr. Woods. Coral did not paint a picture or play a game with Kathy. As the weeks passed, the void progressed to a vacuum. Could we go to the clinic anyway? Maybe we could go just for a visit. Could we at least call the clinic? Certainly we could. But what would we talk about? Would it help Coral? Or more to the point, would it help me?

Thinking rationally, I finally decided that visiting the clinic without an appointment would be awkward, and might even border on being inappropriate—something I'd learned by previous lessons. Gradually it became less of an issue because I simply got used to the new schedule. And I started this writing.

Hope for Tomorrow

Tomorrow is clinic day. Tonight we will make sure Coral gets nothing to eat or drink after midnight in order to facilitate sedation in the morning. She will likely get a bit upset when she figures out that it is clinic day. She will be downright cranky when we deny her breakfast! But we will arrive to a bright and cheerful clinic where she will play with Kathy and an electronic tablet, and board games, and maybe even make a craft. We will talk with our doctors and nurses—our friends—and I will get to review the blood counts and ask questions. The chemo delivery will be completed and Coral will probably wake up from sedation angry as a hornet, as usual. After calming her and feeding her, we will come home and start the monthly process all over again, and this will last another year.

Technically, it's not a cure. It takes a statistical equation and many years of data processing to declare a disease cured. Dr. Schwalm once poignantly scrawled "lifetime" on a form that asked you to indicate the duration of Coral's disease. In general, the current cure rate for ALL is said to be 90 percent. Many factors that differ with each person are considered when giving a prognosis. But what things in life are guaranteed? What things in life offer 90 percent assurance? A quick reference to the not-so-distant past of leukemia, not to mention current and less understood children's cancers, makes 90 percent look phenomenal. Comparatively, in 1953, the year our house was built, the cure rate was literally zero. Precious few if any children survived leukemia. So while this may not be a cure in the eyes of medicine, Coral's durable remission sure feels like one.

Often I think of the adage that if God were to tell us our future, we wouldn't be able to handle it. Our experience with ALL illustrates the truth of that statement. I never would have believed that our family could survive such an event as this. Eileen and Mica share this sentiment with me. Yet, while it may seem impossible to my conscience right now, I would not trade the experience if given the chance. We have grown through the perseverance, although much of it is probably unrealized as of yet. Already we have a new and different perspective and appreciation for life. Surely our worldview has been altered for the better.

One day soon it will be awkward to not administer medications. One day soon "normal" life will truly return. But never will we forget. And never will we take life for granted.

– Shane Meader 2013

Chronology

2012 Timeline

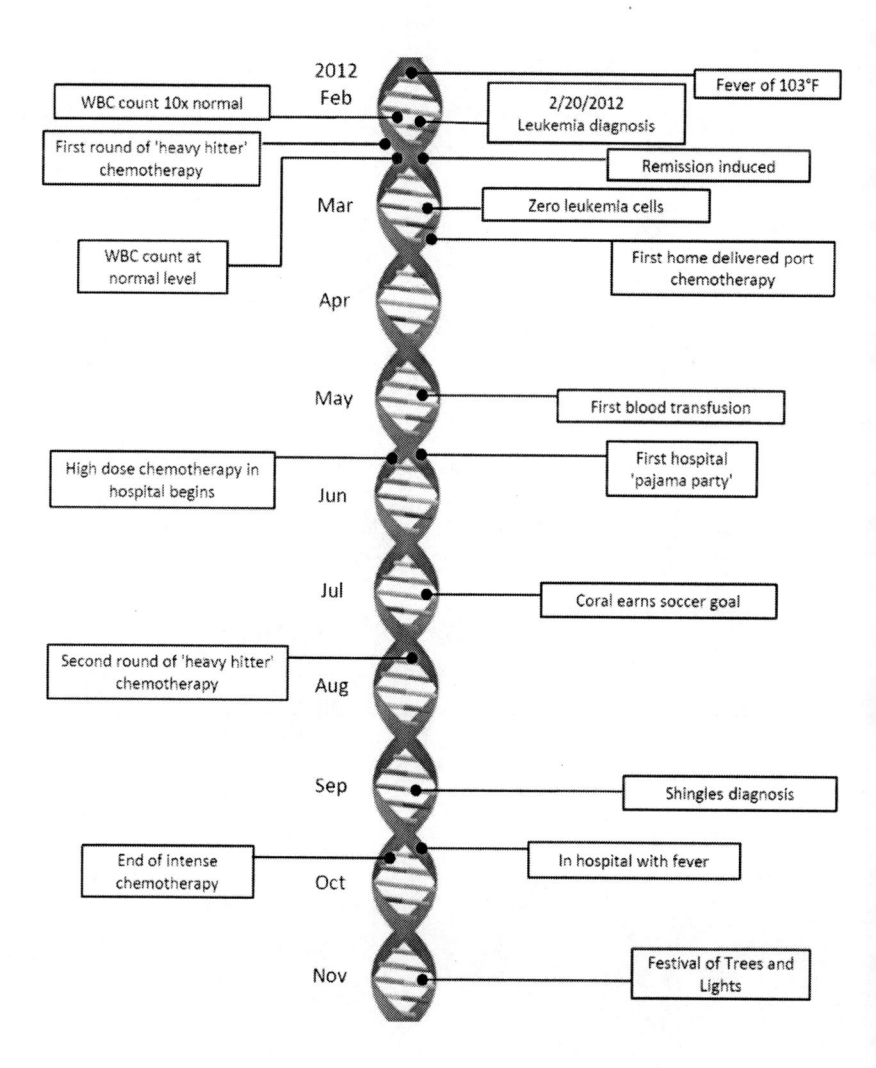

- **Feb 2012**: Fever of 103°F
- **Feb**: WBC count 10x normal
- **2/20/2012**: Leukemia diagnosis
- **Feb**: First round of 'heavy hitter' chemotherapy
- **Feb**: Remission induced
- **Mar**: Zero leukemia cells
- **Mar**: WBC count at normal level
- **Apr**: First home delivered port chemotherapy
- **May**: First blood transfusion
- **Jun**: High dose chemotherapy in hospital begins
- **Jun**: First hospital 'pajama party'
- **Jul**: Coral earns soccer goal
- **Aug**: Second round of 'heavy hitter' chemotherapy
- **Sep**: Shingles diagnosis
- **Oct**: End of intense chemotherapy
- **Oct**: In hospital with fever
- **Nov**: Festival of Trees and Lights

White Cell Count (x1000)

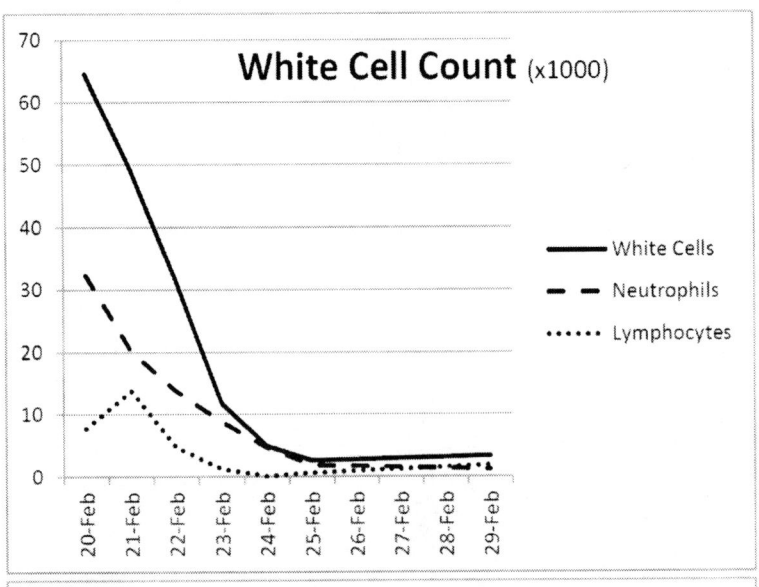

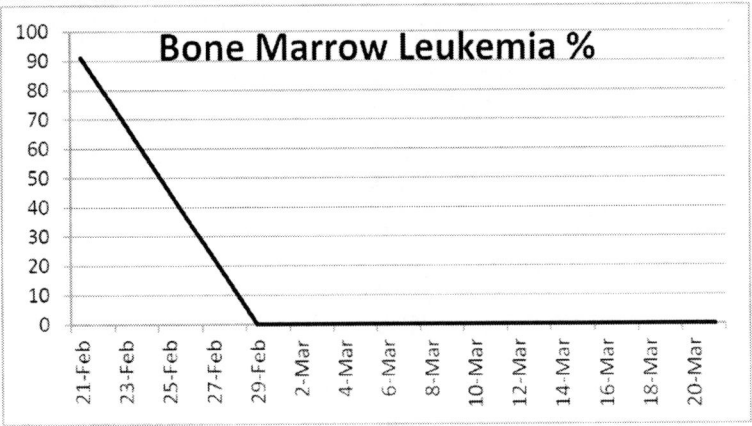

Bone Marrow Leukemia %

Red Cell Count/Hemoglobin

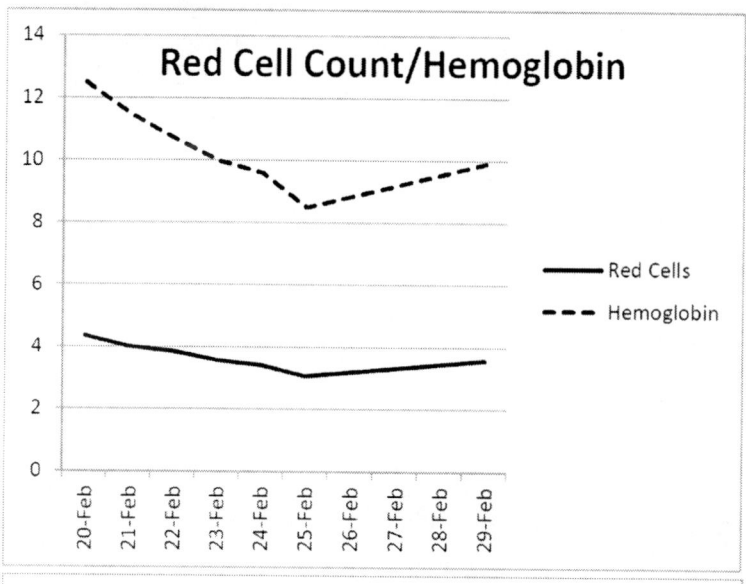

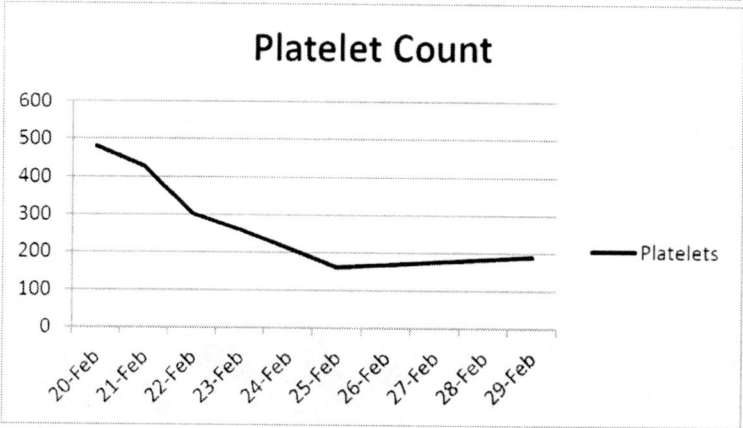

Platelet Count

Appendix

Chemotherapy medication's action from page 40:

Daunorubicin – unwinds and stretches DNA strands creating gaps to fit itself between base pairs. This distortion inhibits DNA replication and repair causing cell death.

Christopher Rokes, M.D., Pediatric Hematologist-Oncologist, Blank Children's Hospital – Causes major reduction in blood counts.

Appendix

Vincristine – binds to microtubules, the building blocks/scaffolding of cell structure, interrupting their assembly and function stopping mitosis.

Dr. Fustino, Dr. Rokes – Real-world observation shows that it does not affect healthy blood cell counts.

Dexamethasone – bolsters/amplifies blood production of the bone marrow, also lethal to leukemic cells.

Dr. Woods – During induction we "amp up" bone marrow blood production with dexamethasone to force out blasts for termination by chemo (this validated my theory for potent steroid use).

Dr. Fustino – Dex has the ability to penetrate CSF (cerebrospinal fluid) and attack blast cells there.

Prednisone – steroid-like dexamethasone with the same action, but much less potent.

Appendix

Cyclophosphamide – forms permanent crosslinks between and within DNA strands which blocks DNA replication leading to cell death.

Cytarabine – cells accept it as a normal DNA component but damages DNA during synthesis.

Methotrexate – an analog for folic acid. Folic acid is needed for chemicals required during DNA synthesis. Cells die from lack of real folic acid.

Mercaptopurine – inhibits synthesis of chemicals required for DNA synthesis.

PEG-asparaginase – breaks down asparagine, a chemical required by cells. Takes advantage of the fact that leukemia cells cannot make asparagine but depend on it created from normal cells.

Appendix

Dr. Fustino – PEG is the anti-asparagine, good cells can recover from the dose, and leukemia cells need much asparagine.

Thioguanine – a guanine analogue, it causes an interference with DNA replication leading to cell cycle arrest and apoptosis.

Dr. Woods – Thioquanine is similar to mercaptopurine inhibiting synthesis of chemicals required by DNA but with the possible side effect of liver injury.

Doxorubicin – similar to and created from daunorubicin but a bit more potent. It relaxes DNA supercoils enabling intercalation during replication. It prevents resealing of the DNA double helix and stops replication.

Dr. Rokes – Usually causes significant nausea.

Appendix

Chemotherapy home delivery instructions from page 86:

Cytarabine (ARA-C) by port

1. Zofran 2.5ml (oral)

2. Clean port tip with alcohol wipe

3. Release tube clamp

4. Flush with 2ml NS (normal saline)

5. Push 2.5ml (50mg) ARA-C over 2 minutes

6. Flush with rest of NS using step 5 rate

7. Flush with 3ml of Heparin

8. Clamp tube

NOTES

The following show some of our questions, answers and notes during treatment.

<u>Concerning the use of glutamic acid:</u>

Should we be administering glutamic acid to reduce the neurotoxicity of vincristine?

Dr. Nick – Glutamic acid would be more for the prevention of neurotoxicity, not for treatment.

Coral has shown no neurotoxicity. Is this evidence of receiving glutamic acid in the clinical trial that we enrolled in?

We are now seeing evidence of vincristine neurotoxicity in Coral's feet. She will get vincristine for many months to come. Wouldn't glutamic acid potentially prevent neurotoxicity for those doses?

Dr. Schwalm – Taking the glutamic acid is fine, many families use it and have good results and swear by it.

Concerning steroid usage:

Why doesn't the roadmap taper off the steroid dosages?

Dr. Nick – Longer steroid treatments do taper off the dosage. We will taper off our dosage if side effects appear – including prednisone during maintenance.

Delayed intensification dexamethasone produced high absolute neutrophil count (ANC) – neutrophil production was not hindered by induction chemo. Why is neutrophil production so high even with doxorubicin and vincristine present? It would seem their rapid division would have made them vulnerable to the chemo meds.

Dr. Rokes – Dexamethasone causes an artificially high ANC (absolute neutrophil count; part of a CBC) because it "knocks them loose" from blood vessel walls and forces them out of the marrow.

Dr. Nick – The precise mechanism of steroids' action on leukemia cells is not well-understood, but its effectiveness has been known for 50 years.

Dexamethasone is more potent than prednisone, dex means "10 times."

Concerning immunizations:

Will she retain any/enough memory B-cells to remember herpes zoster for future suppression?

Dr. Schwalm – No, maybe a few but not enough. We will review her immunizations after treatment.

Should we all get flu shots to help protect Coral?

Dr. Rokes – Yes, even Coral should get one when her numbers come up enough.

Concerning physical therapy:

Why the significant loss of strength, muscle mass, and flexibility from her waist down?

Dr Schwalm – thinks Coral is doing pretty well, foot strength is not that bad, but PT is still a good thing and will help her.

Concerning chemotherapy dosages:

Why adjust 6MP and methotrexate dosage up based upon neutrophil counts (high at 1.83) instead of lymphocyte count (low at .25), pre-B cells are lymphocytes not myelocytes?

Dr. Nick – We use neutrophil count as an indicator/monitor of the effect of chemo on leukemia cells.

Notes

<u>Concerning post treatment:</u>

What do we expect the CBC to look like after maintenance?

Will a detailed bone marrow aspirate and biopsy be performed after therapy?

Dr. Nick – No, bone marrow biopsies should end upon treatment conclusion; CBC is sufficient. Studies have proven that bone marrow biopsies afford no advantage for detecting problems.

What is the percent chance for relapse?

Dr. Nick – 10 percent for all ALL patients. Coral's leukemia was high risk at diagnosis, but the rapid early responder subcategory carries more weight.

When will Coral's port be removed?

Dr. Nick – One month after treatment. Clinic check-ups continue monthly for a year after treatment, including blood draw without the port.

REFERENCES

Baumgartner, B. (photographer). (2012). *Coral Meader wearing mask at Blank Children's Hospital play room (back cover).* [Photograph].

Burgess, J.(Producer). (2004). *The Backyardigans* [Television series]. New York: Nick Jr.

Darabont, F. (Director), & Marvin, N. (Producer). (1994). *The Shawshank redemption* [Motion picture]. United States: Columbia Pictures.

Gojkovich, H. (Executive Producer). (2012, November 21). *News at Five; Festival of Trees and Lights* [Television broadcast]. Des Moines, IA: KCCI.

References

Meader, E. (photographer). (2012). *Coral Meader and Shane Meader sledding at their home (upper cover)*. [Photograph].

Meader, E. (photographer). (2012). *Coral Meader balance beam exercise during physical therapy (back cover)*. [Photograph].

Meader, S. (photographer). (2012). *Coral Meader shown being treated by Wendy Woods-Swafford, M.D. and Child Life Specialist Kathy O'connor at Blank Children's Hospital.* (back cover). [Photograph].

Meader, S. (photographer). (2012). *Coral Meader sedated for intrathecal chemotherapy (back cover)*. [Photograph].

Meader, S. (photographer). (2012). *Coral Meader and Eileen Meader wearing knitted hats (back cover)*. [Photograph].

Meader, S. (photographer). (2012). *Coral Meader wearing clothes basket (back cover)*. [Photograph].

Meader, S. (photographer). (2012). *Coral Meader kicking soccer ball (back cover)*. [Photograph].

Meyer, J. (2011). *Living Beyond Your Feelings*. New York: Hachette Book Group.

REFERENCES

Steinberg, A. (2013, Winter). What cancer has shown me about my little girl. *Cool Kids Connection*, pp. 2, 3.

Wetzel, B. (photographer), Schaefer, H. (photographer). (1982). *Scanning electron microscope image from normal circulating human blood (lower cover)*. [Photograph]. Retrieved from http://commons.wikimedia.org/wiki/File:SEM_blood_cells.jpg

CPSIA information can be obtained at www.ICGtesting.com
Printed in the USA
BVOW03s2159100914

366366BV00012B/74/P